The PARENT- TEACHER PARTNERSHIP

How to Work Together for Student Achievement

SCOTT MANDEL

Zephyr Press

Chicago

Library of Congress Cataloging-in-Publication Data
Mandel, Scott M.
    The parent-teacher partnership : how to work together for student achievement / Scott Mandel.
        p. cm.
    Includes bibliographical references and index.
    ISBN-13: 978-1-56976-217-2
    ISBN-10: 1-56976-217-1
    1. Home and school.   2. Parent-teacher relationships.   3. Academic
       achievement.   I. Title.
    LC225.M317 2007
    371.19′2—dc22

                               2007014311

Cover and interior design: Rattray Design
Front cover image: Jupiterimages
Interior images: © istockphoto.com

© 2007 by Scott Mandel
All rights reserved
Published by Zephyr Press
An imprint of Chicago Review Press,
Incorporated
814 North Franklin Street
Chicago, Illinois 60610
ISBN-13: 978-1-56976-217-2
ISBN-10: 1-56976-217-1
Printed in the United States of America
5 4 3 2 1

This book is dedicated to my children, Aliya and Asher, who grew up to be wonderful young adults without my killing them.

This book is also dedicated to my parents, Bernard and Audrey, who also allowed my siblings and me to do the same.

Contents

Acknowledgments

The production of any book involves the work of many people. First, I want to thank the wonderful people at Zephyr Press and its parent company, Chicago Review Press. Working with them has always been an absolute pleasure! I want to thank my editor, Michelle Schoob, for her brilliant job with my words, and Jerome Pohlen, senior editor, for his assistance in formulating the ideas for this book, and his continuous inspiration and support (along with our annual lunch every summer). I also want to thank Scott Rattray for his beautiful design work on the cover and the interior.

A number of excellent educators and parents in the Los Angeles Unified School District lent their invaluable feedback, ideas, and suggestions to these pages. These people reviewed the material from a variety of different perspectives in the attempt to make this book as valuable as possible to all teachers, administrators, and parents. They are, in alphabetical order: Kathy Anderson, Charlotte Cox, Carl Dugas, Jeanette Hernandez, Robert Krell, Kathie Marshall, and Linda Phillips.

I especially want to thank two awesome educators, Melodie Bitter and Dr. Robert Schuck, who reviewed and provided feedback for each chapter and section throughout the lengthy development and writing process.

Finally, I want to thank the hundreds of teachers and parents who took the time to share their ideas by completing my "Parent-Teacher Partnership: How to Work Together for Student Achievement" questionnaire. Their practical, relevant ideas were critical in writing this book, which is meant for the classroom teacher and parent.

Introduction

Implications of No Child Left Behind

One of the lesser known requirements of the Elementary and Secondary Education Act of 2001, better known as the No Child Left Behind Act (NCLB), is the section pertaining to the School-Parent Compact. This component requires schools to actively include parents in all levels of development and implementation of programs. It mandates that parents become informed and empowered decision makers in the education of their children (Gomez and Greenough 2002). Increased school-parent communication and improved parent support for student achievement are also required. Unfortunately, as with numerous aspects of NCLB, there is no blueprint or model for how to achieve this level of participation.

This new emphasis on parent participation is not a bad thing. While the media has stressed the negative aspects of NCLB, such as the provision allowing students to transfer from low-performing schools, many schools have successfully increased student achievement through positive approaches toward parent involvement, such as the creation of formal partnerships with parents and using a collaborative team model (Ferguson 2005).

The Link Between Parent Involvement and Academic Achievement

Only 15 to 20 percent of the child's waking hours are spent in the school. Therefore, the majority of the child's school-age life comes under the eyes and supervision of the parent, not the teacher. To not include the parent in the child's education ignores the tremendous influence parents hold over the child.

There has been a substantial amount of research on the positive correlation between parents' involvement in their child's education and the subsequent academic achievement of the student (Baker and Soden 1998; Carlson 1991; Epstein 2001; Floyd 1998). The more parents are meaningfully involved in their child's education, the greater achievement demonstrated by the student.

The key to this process is *meaningful involvement*. Getting parents meaningfully involved in the school's educational program does not mean bragging to them at an open house or having Mom or Dad sit and passively listen to an assessment of the child at a parent conference. Rather, meaningful involvement includes:

- Parents and school staff taking an active interest in the well-being of each child, and school staff members taking an interest in the well-being of each child's family as an extension of the child;
- Respecting and valuing families' diverse contributions, and integrating them into the life of the school;
- Encouraging parents to assume multiple roles as supporters, ambassadors, teachers, monitors, advocates, and decision makers;
- Not confining meaningful family involvement to activities that take place in the school building.

(Tellin' Stories Project Action Research Group 2000)

It's All About Attitude

Unfortunately, you can't force teachers and parents to cooperate with each other. Too often the other side is seen as the enemy rather than as a partner. Here are examples of the differences in perspective.

From a classroom teacher's perspective:

- A passive parent is often considered one who "doesn't care about the child's education."
- An active parent is seen as an "aggressive troublemaker."

From a parent's perspective:

- A teacher's "negative" actions are often viewed as a result of "not liking my child."
- A teacher who does not excuse the child from something is giving no consideration to the child's out-of-school life.

Both perspectives are incorrect and too often stereotypical. Both sides need to work together for a common goal—the student's increased academic achievement.

Schools, and the individual teachers on the staff, need to enter into individual partnerships with the parents. Epstein suggests,

> In a caring school community, participants work continually to improve the nature and effects of partnerships. Although the interactions of educators, parents, students, and community members will not always be smooth or successful, partnership programs establish a base of respect and trust on which to build. Good partnerships withstand questions, conflicts, debates, and disagreements; provide structures and processes to solve problems; and are maintained—even strengthened—after differences have been resolved. Without this firm base, disagreements and problems that are sure to arise about schools and students will be harder to solve.

(Epstein 1995, 703)

The central theme of this book focuses on how individual teachers can create positive partnerships with parents, and how individual parents can create positive partnerships with teachers. The majority of the material is classroom centered versus school centered: it concentrates on the day-to-day partnership that should exist between each classroom teacher and each student's parent. More general issues of involving parents in the overall school program are handled beautifully in other books, such as the one written by the National PTA, *Building Successful Partnerships* (2000). These two types of involvement are essential to a successful teacher-parent-school partnership.

Partnerships are a two-way street; one will not succeed without the other. Parents and teachers must partner to improve achievement for all students.

The Model for This Book

The members of a partnership each take separate but equally important roles. The teacher-parent relationship should be viewed in the same way as a doctor-patient relationship. In the latter,

- The doctor is an educated professional, specializing in maintaining the patient's health;
- The doctor provides information for the patient to maintain a normal healthy life;
- The patient comes to the doctor for advice and direction when a problem arises;
- A patient who does not listen to the doctor's advice may experience a less-than-healthy life, to varying degrees;
- A doctor who does not listen to the patient and does not respect the patient's views and background loses that patient's support, and can eventually lose that patient as a client.

Similarly, in a teacher-parent relationship:

- The teacher is an educated professional, specializing in maintaining the student's academic health;

- The teacher provides information for the parent to maintain a healthy academic life for the student;
- The parent comes to the teacher for advice and direction when a problem arises;
- A parent who does not listen to the teacher's advice may experience problems with the student's academic achievement, to varying degrees;
- A teacher who does not listen to the parent and does not respect the parent's views and background loses that parent's support, and in turn can hurt the student's academic achievement.

The material in this book follows this analogy. The teacher is the educated professional working in partnership with the parent with the goal of increasing student academic achievement. The two partners must develop a mutual respect for each other and build on the strengths that each brings to the partnership. The teacher's strength is the educational knowledge developed through years of university schooling and practical teaching experience. The parent's strength is the knowledge of the student's personality, strengths, and weaknesses, as well as the student's home life.

By acknowledging and building on both partners' strengths, this partnership can become truly successful.

The Content and Organization of the Book

The chapters of this book are organized based on the six standards of the National Standards for School-Family-Community Partnership developed by the National PTA in cooperation with the National Coalition for Parent Involvement in Education (NCPIE):

- Standard I: Communicating
- Standard II: Parenting
- Standard III: Student Learning

- Standard IV: Volunteering
- Standard V: School Decision Making and Advocacy
- Standard VI: Collaborating with Community

(National PTA 1998)

Also included is a chapter on the topic of respect, which is critical to fostering a better understanding and partnership between teachers and parents.

The key to this book is its practicality and usability. The concepts center on what the individual classroom teacher and each student's parent can do to create a working, productive partnership. The material is not meant as a basis for a town hall meeting where different parties discuss in generalities how the teacher-parent-school relationship should look. Rather, the ideas presented are meant to be implemented directly into the school, the classroom, and the student's home life on a daily basis.

To make this book as practical and relevant as possible, opinions were gathered from many everyday practitioners—teachers, parents, and administrators—from around the country. The questionnaire distributed to these practitioners included the following open-ended questions:

1. Communication: Describe what you feel teacher-parent communication should be like throughout the school year. Look at it from the perspective of *both* the teacher and the parent.

2. Parenting: What types of parenting help/suggestions can the teacher offer to help parents with their parenting abilities?

3. Student Learning: How can teachers help parents participate more in their students' learning?

4. Volunteering: What are the most helpful/beneficial ways in which parents can assist the teacher through volunteering of time and/or resources?

5. School Decision Making and Advocacy: How can parents best be involved in school decision making and advocacy?

6. Collaborating with the Community: How can teachers best collaborate with the school community?

7. Respect: Please answer as a teacher or parent. What advice/knowledge/insights can you share that will better help teachers respect the parent, or better help the parent respect the teacher?

The responses collected from all stakeholders were used to shape the material in this book, both in its content and its organization.

For the Teacher

Unless otherwise noted, each chapter of this book includes a subsection entitled "For the Teacher." This section explores the issue from the teacher's unique perspective, and suggests ideas and strategies that the teacher can initiate.

At the same time, teachers should also study the subsection entitled "For the Parent." This section explores the issue from the parent's perspective, and suggests ideas and strategies that the parent can initiate. A teacher can use this information in parent workshops or in parent newsletters. Parents who do not actively use these strategies and ideas may not be "unconcerned" or "negative." Rather, they simply may not know how to work in an equal partnership with teachers. Teachers will benefit from sharing this information with their prospective parent partners.

For the Parent

Unless otherwise noted, each chapter of this book includes a subsection entitled "For the Parent." This section explores the issue from the parent's unique perspective, and suggests ideas and strategies that the parent can initiate with the teacher.

At the same time, parents should also study the subsection entitled "For the Teacher." This section explores the issue from the teacher's perspective, and suggests ideas and strategies that the teacher can initiate. Parents can use this information in discussions with their child's teacher. Teachers who do not actively use these strategies and ideas may not be "unconcerned" or "negative." Rather, they may simply not know how to work in an equal partnership with parents—it is not a subject normally covered in education courses. Parents will benefit from sharing this information with their prospective teacher partners.

For the Administrator

All of the information in this book can be shared with teachers through some form of staff development. It also can be shared with parents through workshops or newsletters. The overall goal is to discover and establish ways in which individual classrooms can be improved to create a better atmosphere for meaningful involvement by parents, where parents can serve as partners with teachers working toward improved student achievement, and where teachers view parents as welcome additions to the educational program of the school.

1

Communicating

Mrs. Marshall was frustrated. She wanted to have a conference with Raul Rodriguez's mother about his lack of work, but the mother seemed to be disinterested. Mrs. Rodriguez had not bothered to come in during the scheduled parent-teacher conference the previous week. Notes Mrs. Marshall sent to the Rodriguez home all semester went unanswered. When Mrs. Marshall called the house, Mrs. Rodriguez's English was so poor she did not seem to understand the conversation, so the conversation ended within a minute. Mrs. Marshall sighed—just another parent who didn't care.

Mrs. Rodriguez was frustrated. Her son Raul never seemed to have any schoolwork, and he was receiving poor grades. She couldn't leave her job to go to school for the scheduled parent-teacher conference the previous week, which was held in the afternoon. When she looked through Raul's backpack, she discovered a bunch of notes that his teacher had sent her that he had never bothered to deliver. The teacher called one night, but she was difficult to understand. Mrs. Rodriguez's English was better in person; phone conversations were more difficult. Mrs. Rodriguez sighed. She didn't know how she could help her son succeed in school.

The Issue

Communication is probably the most important issue in the teacher-parent relationship. Communication is certainly the area through which parents have the greatest contact with the school. Positive parent communication almost always results in excellent teacher-parent relationships. Negative, simplistic, or inadequate communication almost always leads to problems throughout the year.

There are two primary types of communication: informational and dialogue. Informational communication is when one side simply informs the other side of something. The content flows one way. It could be as simple as a note sent home or to school. It can be as complex as a formal teacher-parent conference where the teacher and parent are informing each other about the student.

Dialogue is when the two sides share information back and forth for the benefit of the other. The content flows both ways. Too often, all communication between teacher and parent is of the first type—informational—when both types are necessary for a true partnership.

Informational Communication

There are two types of informational communication: personal and impersonal. Personal informational communication primarily happens in the form of teacher-parent conferences—whether scheduled in advance or impromptu. Impersonal informational communication consists mostly of newsletters, Web sites, and other ways of sharing information.

Personal Informational Communication

Traditionally, parent conferences have been the chief way that teachers and parents have interacted. Most are quite productive in sharing important information about the student from both the teacher's and the parents' perspectives. Some are less so. And some could be termed disastrous. Much has been written on how to conduct a successful teacher-parent conference (Mandel 2003). However, a number of principles need to be followed in order to ensure productive, positive communication between teacher and parent.

For the Teacher

The Parent Is an Ally   This is the most important concept that the teacher must grasp. Parents are allies; they want what's best for their child and are willing to work with you toward that goal—if they feel that you have the same motivation. However, if parents see you as a threat to their child, they will instinctively protect their young. If you go into the conference with the idea that the parent wants to work with you, to cooperate with you in helping the child, the likelihood that you'll be viewed as a threat will be extinguished quickly.

The Student Must Be Present at the Conference   I have often canceled a conference if the student was not in attendance. Having the student present is a critical component for any successful conference, especially if you have any negative feedback to share. Too often, a teacher gives negative information to the parents, who then go home and discuss the situation with the child. The child immediately creates excuses or shifts blame—and can be quite convincing. As a result, the parents are put into the awkward position of siding with the teacher or siding with their child. This is especially problematic if it occurs early in the year, before the parents have established a trusting, working relationship with the teacher.

The solution is to always have the student at the conference. (The student should be excused during any portions you or the parents deem sensitive and inappropriate for the child to hear.) Having the child present allows him to give his

Teacher Tip

Parent Contact Outside of School

It is often difficult and inconvenient to try to contact parents during your free period. They are often busy at work, and you are often taking care of things that you need to do. Therefore, consider providing your parents with your e-mail or cell phone number. This will allow parents to get ahold of you outside of school when you have more free time. It is all right to give parents certain parameters, such as "If you e-mail I'll get back to you within forty-eight hours—it may not be immediate" or "Do not call after 10 P.M."

explanations for behaviors or progress in front of the teacher, and in response to the data that the teacher has to share. The student is held accountable for his actions and is forced to take ownership of his academic progress and behaviors. Ultimately, all the parties can forge a solution by discussing the problems faced and the options offered.

Try to not allow school-age siblings in the room during the conference. This is disrespectful to the student. Siblings will often use the information they hear against the student, which may cause problems at home.

Be Flexible with Your Hours   Often teachers view parents who do not come for conferences as uninterested in their child's school life. While this is sometimes the case, it isn't so the majority of the time, especially when dealing with a population in a lower-income area. Very often both parents work, and work in an hourly wage or other position where they would be forced to take off the entire day. For these parents, taking a day off or leaving work for a conference can be stressful or even an economic burden.

The rule of thumb is if parents can't make one of your times, make one of theirs. This may mean an occasional 7 A.M. or 5 P.M. conference. Yes, it may be an inconvenience, but establishing the partnership with that parent will provide much more benefit than skipping the conference. In addition, demonstrating your flexibility will go a long way in the eyes of the parent.

Adapt to Language and Cultural Differences   Arrange to have a translator present for conferences with parents who are not fluent in English. Without a translator, not only will the parents be unable to have a dialogue with you about the student, but you may subtly imply that their participation in their child's schooling is irrelevant. If the parents are not in a position where they can freely and completely share their thoughts due to a language barrier, then you will not have true communication, much less a partnership.

Occasionally, parents supply their own translator, such as an older sibling or a family friend. Sometimes you may need to arrange with the school to provide an aide or some other translator. Make arrangements ahead of time, not when the parent shows up. If you aren't sure whether parents are fluent in English, ask the student beforehand.

It is also important that you strive for unambiguous communication and refrain from using educational jargon. This is a good general practice for most conferences. However, when the parent is not fluent in English, it is even more important. Watch for embarrassment from the parents if they seem to not understand what you are saying. Embarrassment is an extremely negative emotion, one that might poison any potential working relationship you want to establish with the parents.

Be aware of cultural differences—these can often lead to misinterpretations or awkwardness. For example, in America a firm handshake is expected as a sign of confidence and respect. However, in some Latin American cultures, handshakes are expected to be "weak," almost as if the hands are simply touching. This is *not* a sign of weakness; it's merely a cultural difference. Another common mistake is when a teacher sends a note to Asian American parents. Names written in red are a sign of death in these cultures, so avoid using red ink in your notes.

One schoolwide program that can really help communication is a parent coordinator/parent liaison program. A parent coordinator serves as a communication pathway between teachers and parents, especially when there are language or cultural differences within the school population. This person can in-service teachers on areas of cultural concern and help arrange adequate translation assistance when necessary.

Being aware of and adapting to language and cultural differences will go a long way toward establishing a positive relationship with the parents.

Adapt to the New American Family   In twenty-first-century American society, it is quite probable that a significant percentage of your students do not live with both of their biological parents. Divorced and remarried parents are beginning to become the norm. This not only puts increased stress on the child but on the teacher, as another variable comes into play in home-school issues. Here are some pointers to consider when dealing with conferencing with these households:

- Whenever possible, have all parties—including stepparents—at the conference. This helps ensure that everyone is on the same page, and there is less of a chance of the child pitting one parent or stepparent against another.
- When the two parents cannot conference together, set up two separate conferences. This is critical if the child is spending time with both. The parent left out will almost always become less supportive, to the point of sabotaging what you are attempting to do with the child.
- Always include the stepparent. He or she is an intricate part of the home life, and the student needs to see the stepparent showing an interest and being supportive.
- Help make their situation better. Often the student will play one parent against the other and try to manipulate the situation to his advantage.

Remind the parent to be aware of what is happening, and whenever possible, confront the child with the other parent present. Let them know that they must present a united front—this is critical, even if it is the only thing that the two parents agree on! You can also help avoid potential problems. For example, if there is shared physical custody, assign the student an extra set of books to keep at each parent's house.

- Do not get involved in their negative issues. If the parents try to get you to take a side, refuse. Immediately stop any conversation that strays to negative talk about the other parent. If a parent insists that the other parent is not legally entitled to participate, ask to see the court order stating this. If this is not produced, you are under the obligation to inform both sides of student information.

For the Parent

Conferencing Is a Two-Way Street   It is the parents' responsibility to stay on top of their child's education. There should never be surprises at teacher-parent conference time. You should have a very good idea where your child is—academically and behaviorally—before you ever get to the conference. The meeting time should then be used to develop and agree on strategies to help your child's progress.

You should be keeping track at home of what is going on in school and regularly monitoring your child's work. If you rarely see assignments coming home, chances are it is not a matter of the teacher not assigning work. More likely, your child is purposely disposing of assignments before you can see them. Let the teacher know that you have not seen any work for a while. Regularly ask your child when upcoming tests or projects are due. If you do not get a satisfactory answer, contact the teacher by phone, note, or e-mail.

The Teacher Only Knows Half of the Story   When teachers give assignments, they have a good idea of how long they should take, based on the material and their knowledge of their students. This is not a hard-and-fast rule. Sometimes there are unforeseen difficulties.

If your child is having difficulty with an assignment—it is taking an abnormal amount of time, or there is a comprehension problem—send the teacher a private note explaining the situation, in a sealed envelope or by e-mail. The key word here is "abnormal." If it always takes your child two hours to do a certain type of homework, or if she continually has difficulties understanding the material, that is a different situation, which may require a conference. However, if your child takes two hours to complete an assignment when she normally takes thirty minutes, or if your child suddenly is unusually frustrated, let the teacher know.

Please note, this does not mean you should send the teacher notes to relieve your child of assignments or excuse a poor grade. This note is informational; it lets the teacher know that something about this particular assignment is abnormal and that the teacher may want to look into the situation.

Keep the Teacher Informed About the Student's Life Outside of School   It is critical that you keep your child's teacher informed of problems or situations in

Parent Tip
Getting Rid of the TV Temptation

Make a policy in your home: no television on school nights, period. Too often when you tell your children they can watch TV after they finish their homework, they *will* hurry up and finish—and do an inadequate job. If they know they are not going to watch television no matter what, they may tend to do a better job on their work, and maybe even do something constructive such as read a book after they finish. Let them tape their shows during the week and watch them on the weekend. (My own children used to have a stack of VCR tapes to watch at 7 A.M. every Saturday morning.)

your child's life that may affect him at school. These might be long-term situations or they might involve one particular day. Here is a true story:

A student was often misbehaving. Some days, he seemed to be "off the wall" and extremely difficult to control. As a result, the teacher regularly gave him negative consequences for his behavior, especially on his bad days. In April, the mother nonchalantly informed the teacher that the child would be leaving school early one day because his doctor wanted to change his medication. The teacher looked at the parent in surprise and asked, "What medication?" She never knew—because the parent never informed her—that the student was diagnosed with ADHD, and on those bad days, he had forgotten to take his medication. If the teacher had been aware that his misbehavior was a result of a condition and was not voluntary, she would have handled him differently.

It is imperative that you inform the teacher as soon as possible of situations like the ones in the following list. This list is not exhaustive by any means, but it should give you an idea of the type of information that should be shared. All of these items affect your child in school and, more importantly, will affect how the teacher reacts to any change in the child's behavior.

- **Parents separating or divorcing.** The teacher should be informed as soon as the child learns about an impending divorce or separation, and again when the divorce or separation is finalized. All children become depressed or anxious to an extent at this time, and the school has resources that can help the child cope during this extremely emotional period. At a minimum, the teacher should be sympathetic to the child and inform you of any personality changes.
- **Severe illness or death of a close family member.** Again, students are very concerned and anxious when a close family member is ill or passes away. Concentration on work significantly diminishes, and the child might act out. An informed teacher can be understanding and help the child through this period.

- **Family economic problems.** When a parent loses a job or some other economic catastrophe occurs, the child usually feels the resulting stress from the parents. The child might worry about losing her home, missing out on activities, or even having enough food to eat.

- **Child is on medication or has a condition that affects learning.** Teachers should immediately know if a child has ADD/ADHD or any other condition that may affect schoolwork or behavior. Teachers should also be aware if the child has just been prescribed glasses—often children won't wear them in front of their friends.

- **Child did not get normal sleep.** Sometimes family emergencies prevent a child from getting adequate sleep. Send a note or call the teacher—that way, the teacher can help the child cope with that day's responsibilities.

- **Major fight/disagreement in the morning.** If your child has had a major fight or disagreement with you or another family member in the morning before school, the resulting anger might be directed toward the teacher or others at school. Sharing this information with the teacher puts her on alert to emotions the student should keep in check at school.

Impersonal Informational Communication

Impersonal informational communication refers to information about the school or classroom that is sent home to parents, and vice versa. It is difficult for parents to get involved with a school program if they do not have information about it. Problems can arise when communication from the home to the classroom is mishandled.

For the Teacher

Beginning of the Year Communication In the first week of the school year, it is critical that teachers communicate classroom philosophies and student expectations to parents. Most schools have a type of "Back to School Night" some time in the first month of the new school year. However, by this time weeks have gone by—and not every parent is able to attend. Therefore, make contact early in the year to assure that parents sign onto your educational program. There are two excellent ways to do this:

- **Welcoming newsletter.** Send a welcoming newsletter to parents within the first two days of school. In this newsletter, include both your overall philosophy and your expectations. Include types of homework and projects, late homework policies, and other information the parents should know. Most importantly, be sure to ask parents to sign a short note affirming that they received and read the newsletter. This will help if later in the year, a parent says, "I didn't know . . . ."

- **Phone calls.** Phone calls to each parent take some time but are extremely worthwhile. When parents were surveyed in preparation for this book, most responded that they want the teacher's "personal touch." Calling parents at the beginning of the year will help you forge a positive relationship with them immediately. The calls should be short, no more than a few minutes each (you can spend under fifteen minutes by making just four or five calls a night). Even secondary teachers with 150 students can complete the calls over a few weeks. The call should be simple: "Hello, this is _____, your child's teacher. I just wanted to call and introduce myself, and see if you have any questions about the newsletter I sent home." Usually the parents won't have any questions, but if they do, you can immediately clear up any misunderstandings before they become a serious problem.

Ongoing Communication   Throughout the year, provide parents with information about events or projects. Letting parents know when a new unit is going to begin can assist them in supporting your curricular program at home. Periodic newsletters are a great way to supply this information. A new tool gaining popularity is classroom/teacher Web sites. Your school may already have this available. If not, you can set up a Web site and e-mail address through a number of online companies. Most charge a small fee, but an excellent free service is available through these two sites: ClassNotes Online (www.classnotesonline.com) and Yourhomework.com (www.yourhomework.com).

However, be aware that some families do not have Internet access. You can get this information unobtrusively by adding a private question on a test or assignment: "Do you currently have Internet access?" For families without access, make handouts of the Web site and either mail them to parents or have students take them home. Another type of ongoing communication involves informing parents about the progress of children with academic or behavioral problems. A short weekly progress report, that you ask the parent to sign, is an excellent way to keep parents up-to-date on their child's progress. The progress report can be something as simple as writing a "smiley" or "frowning" face in an academic diary (a student calendar specially designed with daily spaces to write in assignments). Or use a blank form with a scale you can quickly fill in, such as this:

	Great		Fair		Poor
Behavior	5	4	3	2	1
Classwork	5	4	3	2	1
Homework	5	4	3	2	1

Teacher Signature _____

Parent Signature _____

Comments: _____

_____

_____

_____

_____

_____

Either way, you can apprise parents of their child's progress without having to schedule additional conferences.

Soliciting Parent Information   Some parents have no difficulty telling you what they think or feel. However, the majority find it hard to deliver feedback. Since feedback can be extremely beneficial, teachers should actively solicit parent information. One way to do this is through the use of periodic parent surveys. Usually parent surveys are used to discover parent strengths and whether or not they can help with certain events or projects. But they can also be used to solicit parents' opinions of their child's activities. For example, if there is a curricular-type event that parents attend, survey their opinions as to whether they felt welcome, enjoyed it, thought that their child learned, and so on.

This type of solicitation gives you important feedback, makes the parents feel like they have a stronger partnership with you, and most important, gives that personal touch that parents want. However, if you receive certain strong opinions or concerns from individual parents, make sure to ask yourself if they are reflective of the needs of all.

For the Parent

Providing Information to the Teacher   In addition to conferences, parents can use personal notes to supply the teacher with the information necessary to help deal with a child. Sometimes writing notes is difficult, especially in the hectic morning hours. However, the information you provide can assist the teacher greatly.

There are a couple of issues parents should take into serious consideration when sending a written communication to the teacher:

■ Personal information should always be sent in a sealed envelope or an e-mail. Too often parents send notes containing information that the child should not read. A student will most likely read an unsealed note—personal

Parent Tip

Getting Rid of the TV Temptation

Make a policy in your home: no television on school nights, period. Too often when you tell your children they can watch TV after they finish their homework, they *will* hurry up and finish—and do an inadequate job. If they know they are not going to watch television no matter what, they may tend to do a better job on their work, and maybe even do something constructive such as read a book after they finish. Let them tape their shows during the week and watch them on the weekend. (My own children used to have a stack of VCR tapes to watch at 7 A.M. every Saturday morning.)

curiosity and fear of getting into trouble take over. This is especially true if your child has a problem with the classroom or teacher. By letting your child read the note, she might feel empowered and assume that you will automatically take her side against the teacher. As a result, she might demonstrate a negative attitude toward the teacher that day, which may escalate the original problem.

■ Style is critical. Just as a teacher must choose his words carefully when conferencing with parents, parents also must consider how they word their notes. Teachers are human, and they react as any person will when they feel threatened or insulted. If you have a problem with something connected to the classroom or teacher, the language in your note will affect how the teacher will react and how he will perceive you in the future. For example:

  ■ *Don't say:* "This grade is unfair. My daughter didn't deserve a *D*."
  ■ *Say:* "I have some questions about the last test. Can you contact me tonight?"
  ■ *Don't say:* "My son doesn't have time to do this project. We can't get to the library."

■ *Say:* "We have some problems with this project. Can you give me a call so we can figure out some solutions?"

In both instances, you are letting the teacher know that you have concerns and are asking for feedback and information, without automatically putting the teacher on the defensive and branding yourself a "problem parent."

Dialogic Communication

Dialogic communication differs from informational communication in that the material flows back and forth for the betterment of both parties. This type of communication is critical for establishing a full teacher-parent partnership designed to improve the school and classroom, and ultimately the child's academic program. Dialogic communication is based on the teacher, as the educational professional, and the parent, as the involved partner, wanting to learn more to help the child succeed. Both the teacher and the parents need to view parents as active learners who want to be involved to ensure their children's academic progress.

The National Education Longitudinal Study (1988) looked at what types of parental involvement in the child's school life made the greatest difference in the child's academic achievement. Of the four main areas of parent involvement studied—home discussion, home supervision, school communication, and school participation—the study determined that home discussion was the most important variable. In order for parents to be able to have home discussion with their children concerning the academic program, they must have an established dialogue with the teacher.

For the Teacher

Establishing Trust   It is primarily the responsibility of the teacher to establish a level of trust with parents, so parents will want to learn from the teacher. Look at parents as partners, and do not be condescending. The situation is similar to that of a teacher who leads an in-service class for her teacher peers. All parties are equal in status. One, however, has certain knowledge that is to be shared with the others.

A good way to establish this is with an open-door policy in your classroom. An open-door policy means parents are welcome to drop in and observe your classroom at any time, without an appointment. This makes parents feel welcome and shows them that your teaching is open to observation. Obviously, you should establish some limits:

- **Inappropriate times.** There are some times when parents will not be able to drop in. For example, visitors should not be allowed during testing periods because of the distraction they may cause.
- **Abuse of privilege.** Parents who visit more than once every few weeks may be abusing your policy. You need to decide on responsible limits on visitation, based on frequency and parents' motivation.
- **Hidden agendas.** Some parents have hidden agendas, and their visitations are planned to acquire certain information—often at the teacher's detriment. If you suspect this, discuss it with the parent or an administrator and then limit the visitations.

Determining How You Can Help Holding a parent workshop in the evening—even if it is on your own time—is often beneficial to your classroom program. Early in the year, I always conduct a homework workshop for parents. In this session, I describe the different types of homework assignments their children will have. More important, I teach them how to help, and *not* help, their children. I assist them in setting boundaries at home so they can become supporters of my academic program.

To help parents be more supportive of your program, introduce them to curricular areas so they know what their child will be learning. This is especially helpful before you begin large units where a significant final project is assigned. You can send home an introductory information sheet, a graphic organizer, or some other type of information to provide parents with an introduction to the subject matter to be studied.

You can also help parents by providing them with other curricular information. Send syllabi home so parents can keep abreast of what their child is learning. Provide parents with a list of Web sites that correspond to the current unit. The parents can look at the sites on their own and research pertinent areas that follow the curriculum. For example, you can send the following paper to parents before a new unit on American history: Immigration.

We are about to study American immigration between 1880 and 1920. The following are some Web sites where you can find related information, which you can then discuss with your child:

Immigration—Their Stories
library.thinkquest.org/20619/Past.html
   Lots of information on the immigrant experience—who immigrants were, why they came, and issues that they faced.

Ellis Island Foundation
www.ellisisland.org
   Lots of information and pictures from the museum on Ellis Island. Be sure to click on the "Ellis Island" link on the top.

Even if English is not the parent's first language, a vast amount of curricular material is available in various languages. For example, most textbooks have Spanish editions, and the school may be able to lend a copy to a parent. And, virtually any page on the Internet can be translated into dozens of different languages.

For the Parent

Learn for Your Sake, Learn for Your Child's Sake　You are the most important role model for your child. If you keep up with the basic information that your child is learning, she will see that education is important on all levels. By being familiar with the curriculum (expertise is not required, just familiarity), you are also better equipped to monitor and help with your child's progress through assignments, projects, and exams.

Concerning this concept, a parent wrote:

> I do this with my kids and very often I can clarify questions they have that they may feel embarrassed to ask in class. Sometimes the teacher needs to move on before my children have completely grasped an idea. Learning their material and supporting them when needed tells them that I will not leave them twisting in the wind.
>
> (Mandel, 2006b)

Browse through your child's textbook and familiarize yourself with the material. You can find similar material on an adult level online to accomplish the same thing. In addition, ask your child's teacher to provide or suggest some curricular materials that you can read to gain familiarity with the subjects your child is learning.

If English is not your first language, there is much curricular material available in various languages. As stated in the teacher section, most textbooks have Spanish editions. The school may be able to lend you a copy. Additionally, virtually any page on the Internet can be translated into dozens of different languages.

Share Your Interests with Your Child's Teacher　If there is an area in which you are interested, share that with the teacher. Even if the area is not part of your child's curriculum, the teacher can serve as an educational resource who can either provide you with materials or direct you to them.

Remember, parents are the number-one role models for their children. If your child sees that education—active learning—is important to you, it will be that much more important in your child's eyes.

2

Parenting

Mrs. Andrews was frustrated. Tiffany was repeatedly late to first period and always had to catch up with the discussion. Every time Mrs. Andrews talked to Tiffany's parents, they always had some excuse for Tiffany's lack of work or for her inappropriate behavior. There seemed to be no consequences at home, and Tiffany knew this, using the situation to her full advantage. Mrs. Andrews sighed—just another parent who didn't know how to parent.

Mrs. Johnson was frustrated. Her daughter Tiffany always argued about everything, ignored what her mother said, and then did whatever she wanted. Getting Tiffany ready for school in the morning was a battle, getting her to do her homework was a battle, and getting her to do chores at home was a battle. Whenever Mrs. Johnson tried to establish some limits, Tiffany would shout that she hated her. Mrs. Johnson desperately did not want to turn out like her own mother, so she usually backed down to her daughter, hoping that it was simply a phase Tiffany was going through. Mrs. Johnson sighed—why didn't she ever learn how to parent a teenager?

The Issue

Hundreds of questionnaires from parents, teachers, and administrators were collected in the research for this book. Of all the topics addressed, none provided more diverse and strong opinions than the question:

> What types of parenting help/suggestions can the teacher offer to help parents with their parenting abilities?

> (Mandel 2006b)

Responses from both teachers and parents ranged from asking for/offering help in every area of parenting or the school's curricula to statements proclaiming that parenting is solely the parent's business and the teacher should stay completely out of it.

The answer is probably somewhere in between. This chapter takes the position that parenting is the parents' responsibility, and the teacher is the parents' number-one resource.

One questionnaire response stated that "99 percent of parenting is *ad hoc*"—made up on the spot. In many ways this is true. Professionals in every field attend dozens of classes to earn degrees or pass certain established requirements to gain credentials or licenses. Manual laborers need to learn how to operate machinery or perform other facets of their jobs. But anyone can be a parent. No classes, licensing, or anything else is required. Ph.D.'s and day laborers—few, if any, have had any courses or formal training in how to practice good parenting skills.

This book does not consider whether adults are good or bad at parenting. Instead, it focuses on whether parents are informed or not informed. And that is a critical difference. There are no value judgments—just ideas to consider, or not.

This chapter is divided into two major sections: Parenting Skills and Supporting the School's Curriculum. Parents can study these ideas on their own; teachers can share them with their students' parents. The ideas are not exhaustive but are meant to be considered as both groups—teachers and parents—work together as partners to help children be the best they can be, in all aspects of their lives, now and later as responsible, productive adults.

Parenting Skills

Attitude is crucial when dealing with parenting skills. Teachers cannot be judgmental, and parents cannot see them as such. The teacher has expertise on children's development gleaned through his years of education and experience. The parents have hands-on experience and, even more important, a vested interest in good parenting skills. Teachers and parents must work together in order to be truly successful.

Unlike the previous chapter, this particular section is not divided into separate "For the Teacher" or "For the Parent" sections. All of the information in this chapter is applicable to both parents and teachers—whether parents read this material for themselves or the teacher shares the ideas through a workshop or other printed material.

Consider the presentation of this information as a learning experience similar to teacher in-service sessions. In a teacher in-service session, the workshop leader, who is educated in some specific area, shares expertise with the teachers. The teachers adapt what is relevant to their classroom situation and leave the rest. Similarly, parents should consider the ideas presented in this chapter, adapt what they feel is appropriate for their home situation, and discard the rest. What parents get out of this material will vary. However, the goal is to raise the level of good parenting for the benefit of the children.

For the Teacher and the Parent

The Parents Themselves   As many baby boomers became adults, they desperately attempted to treat their children differently than their often-strict parents had treated them. They were more lenient and protective than any previous generation of parents. Unfortunately, this philosophy has been taken to the extreme by the now-adult children of baby boomers. As parents, this generation (sometimes called Generation X), has all too often gone to new extremes for the perceived betterment of their children, over all other considerations (Gibbs 2005).

It is critical that parents today understand the following philosophy concerning their children:

- You are their parents, not their friends.
- You are their parents, not their "personal manager."
- You are their parents, and their primary role model.

You can have a wonderful, friendly relationship with your children. You can help guide them with their personal decisions. You may become best friends as adults, but as your children are growing up, you need to be a parent. You need to make the decisions necessary to ensure their growth into successful and self-sufficient human beings. Sometimes that means making decisions that may not be popular and, when your children are older, letting them learn and grow from their mistakes.

Here are some thoughts to guide you through parenting children today:

- **You are your child's primary role model.** Your behavior—both positive and negative—sets the example for your children. Cursing, allowing your child to make excuses for her behaviors, even double-parking in illegal zones at school, give subtle messages to your child. At the same time, the opposite behaviors—acting with character in all dealings concerning your children or in their presence—will equally be noticed.

Over the last few years, schools have increasingly instituted "character education" programs. These programs teach the Six Pillars of Character: trustworthiness, respect, responsibility, fairness, caring, and citizenship (Josephson 1993).

However, as wonderful and interesting as these programs are, nothing the school attempts in this area will be as effective as you being a role model—positively or negatively—in your child's character development.

Singer-songwriter Harry Chapin's song "Cat's in the Cradle" (1974) goes through stages in a boy's life where the father is too busy to spend much time with his son. In the final verse, when the son is too busy to spend time with his retired father, the father discovers a startling revelation: "And as I hung up the phone it occurred to me, my boy was just like me. My boy was just like me."

Like it or not, you as parents have the responsibility of being the most significant, and influential, role model for your children.

■ **Attitude is everything.** Teachers know that there is such a thing as a self-fulfilling prophecy. This is when students raise or lower themselves to the teacher's expectations. If the teacher expects the child to do well, she often does. If she expects that she will not, she often does not. Children innately want to please supervisory adults, be they teachers or parents. And to a child, there is no better way to please the adult than to do what is expected, positively or negatively, consciously or unconsciously. Of course, this does not work in all situations, nor with all students. However, it happens often enough that it is important to be aware of this phenomenon.

The self-fulfilling prophecy is applicable to the home as well. If you have high expectations, if you emphasize achievement, chances are better that your child will aspire toward that goal. Letting the child get away with the statement "I tried my best" will often lead to the opposite scenario.

What is the child's "best"? Only you and the teacher know. Look at the best work, or the best behavior, that your child demonstrates throughout the year and use that as the benchmark for the "best." For example, if your child gets two *A*s, five *C*s, and two *D*s on his math quizzes, you know that he is capable of earning *A*s. That is his "best." Now that the benchmark has been established, you can work with him to determine what it was that brought him the *A*s—and conversely, the *C*s and *D*s. But *you* determine what is acceptable, and you know whether your child is actually doing his best.

■ **Get help when needed.** As stated earlier, there are few courses in good parenting skills. There is no advance credentialing. Most of parenting is learning as you go. You probably tried different strategies on your second child than on your first (and your oldest child will quickly verify this if asked).

Use your child's teacher as a resource. If you need advice on how to handle your child in a certain situation, the teacher may have knowledge in that area gleaned from years of experience. The teacher also may have resources you can consult to find answers. There are two points to remember:

■ *First, you do not have to take the teacher's advice.* Listen to it and then decide how it fits in with your home situation. Ultimately, you, as the parent, are the one to make the final decision.

■ *Second, asking for advice is not a sign of weakness or failure.* Quite the contrary—it demonstrates that you are aware of what parenting information you know and what you do not know, and that you are willing to seek the best answers. This is common practice when you want medical advice, legal advice, and financial advice. There is nothing wrong with seeking parenting advice.

Home Life

This section centers on what you establish for your child within your home. It is also the area where you experience the majority of arguments and resistance from your child. Through it all, remember *you* are the parent, and *you* are the one making the ultimate decisions. Families are not meant to be democracies. They are benevolent dictatorships. You care deeply about your charges, but you are the one making the final decisions based on what you feel is best for your child's welfare.

- **Children need routines.** Adults have routines throughout their home life. Getting ready for work, doing laundry, cooking, cleaning the house, paying bills, weekends—all are governed to some point by specific routines. Children also need routines in their lives to give them direction and teach them responsibility. Routines should govern what your child does in the morning before school, what she does after school, homework, even weekend chores and activities to an extent. Children need to accept responsibilities. This prepares them not only for success in school but also for later family life when they are on their own.

- **The parent is responsible for the child's personal welfare.** You need to ensure that your child is kept clean and healthy. You are ultimately responsible for what your child eats and what exercise he receives.

    An excellent documentary was recently produced entitled *Super Size Me* (Spurlock, educationally enhanced edition 2004). In this film, the director ate nothing but McDonald's for one month—breakfast, lunch, and dinner. The film, however, is about much more than his deteriorating health from a fast food diet (which was appalling). The basic premise of the material concerns the state of the youth in America today—overweight and/or out of shape. It is quite specific and disturbing. However, it is a movie that every parent and child should see together, followed by a discussion of the child's life habits.

■ **The parent is the ultimate supervisor.** In today's busy world, this certainly isn't easy, nor is it always pleasant. But you are the one who ultimately supervises your child's life. This does not just mean things like getting your child to school on time (though that is an important component of your child's success in school). It deals with how your child interacts with the outside world.

We live in a somewhat frightening world today. Reports of online sexual predators seem to be increasing, and our children are much more sophisticated in adult areas such as language or sex than ever before. Parents should supervise their children with regard to the following:

■ *How is your child dressed for school?* Increasingly, pre-teen and teenage girls are wearing clothes with plunging necklines, bare midriffs, and suggestive language. This type of clothing can lead to problems, as boys as early as elementary age become more aggressive toward girls wearing suggestive clothing. You as a parent need to monitor what your child wears to school. Check your child's wardrobe—and backpack—before she leaves for school. Is she bringing something to change into once she leaves the house? Is she wearing a sweatshirt or coat zipped up (hiding the clothes underneath) on a day that does not seem to warrant it? Is he sneaking gang-related clothing or accessories, or wearing shirts with inappropriate words?

■ *How much time does your child spend on the computer?* Do you know what he is doing online? This is simply good parenting. Our parents used to ask us where we were going and who we were going with. Children today seem to do most of their socializing online. The same questions should be asked about this time online.

■ **Children want love and support.** This does not mean that you should spoil your child. Getting upset with or punishing a child for inappropriate behavior or actions actually demonstrates to your child that you care enough to act. To a child, negative attention is better than no attention.

One of the hardest things for a parent to do, especially in today's society, is let children make their own mistakes and live with them. I am not talking about health-threatening mistakes. Children need to learn how to make decisions, and then how to live with the positive—or negative—consequence of those decisions. This is critical for learning how to act as an adult, and how to deal with the life choices that they will be required to make. Taking responsibility is a skill—and skills need to be practiced. Sometimes your children will make poor choices, and as a parent, you will want to save them. But if you always save your children from mistakes, how will they ever learn?

Taking the time to give your children both positive and negative feedback demonstrates to them that you care about and are interested in their lives. It gives them positive self-esteem, and more important, it teaches them how to be a caring parent later on. Remember, you are your child's primary role model in this department.

Having the attention of a parent is important to the child's development. This is especially important for elementary age children, and for children of two working parents. Try to find a set time every week, or every day if possible, for "special time." This is an unbreakable appointment with your child, where the child decides what you two will do together. It may be as simple as reading a story or playing a game at night. It may be going to the park together for a couple of hours on the weekend. Whatever it is, it demonstrates to your child that she is so important that no matter how busy you are, you can give her your time.

Supporting the School's Curriculum

I have rarely met parents who did not want their child to succeed in school. Unfortunately, most parents are not taught *how* to best help their children succeed.

> Reading aloud to your children and letting them see you reading are two of the best ways to help them on the road to literacy.
>
> (Macfarlane 1994)

This section centers on how parents can actively support the school's curriculum to ensure their child's success. A child's success in school cannot be assumed to be solely the teacher's domain. To the contrary, a full partnership between the classroom teacher and the parent is essential to a successful school life for the child.

For the Teacher

Homework Help   Parents cannot assist their child with homework if they are not taught the correct, and incorrect, way of doing so. This is where you enter the picture. Teaching parents how to help with homework does not mean teaching them the curricular material. Rather, you need to teach them the best ways to support your program at home.

Taking one evening in the first month or two of the school year and holding a Parent Homework Night is an excellent way to deliver your message. In this workshop, you can talk about the types of assignments you give, what the assignments require, and how parents can work with their child. For example, here are some common homework tips to share with parents:

- Check to make sure that what the child does is what is assigned. Have your child write his assignments in an "academic diary" or other form of assignment book. (Academic diaries can be purchased online at www.actionagendas.com.) Insist that your child write the entire assignment, such as "page 47, #1–20" rather than just "page 47." This will reduce confusion in the subsequent parent/child discussion that evening.
- Do not give your child the correct answers, no matter how hard she begs or tries to manipulate you. If your child hands you the book and says, "The

Teacher Tip

A Homework Policy Based on Student Responsibility

I have a special homework policy for my students to teach them responsibility and time-management techniques. This policy also assists during parent conferences where I insist that the student take responsibility for the grades.

Most of my students are average to above-average in ability. My assignments in English and history are primarily comprehension question assignments. The students normally are given two to three days to complete these particular assignments (not tests, spelling assignments, and other specific work). The following policies are in effect for these specific assignments.

- These assignments may be turned in late with no penalty. This is for the benefit of the students who are extremely diligent with their work, and who will stay up until 10 or 11 P.M. to finish. It takes pressure off them when they occasionally are so busy that they cannot do so without some personal sacrifice. However, the students who misuse this policy quickly fall so far behind that they cannot catch up without spending entire weekends on their work.

- These assignments may be redone for a better grade, which is the one recorded. Sometimes students may have difficulty with an assignment, or some outside force causes them to do less than their best work. This is extremely stressful for some of the higher students. By letting them redo poor grades (or even a B in order to receive an A), the students better learn the material. They can examine what they did incorrectly and improve upon it, ultimately learning the material.

The beauty of this system is that all of the responsibility is on the student, and not on you. When the parent discovers that:

1. Missing work could have been completed late, turned in for full credit, *and*
2. Poor grades could have been corrected and turned in for a better grade

The parent is really upset—but not at you. At the student. Students and parents learn that the only way someone receives a *D* or an *F* in my class is if they basically say, "I'm not going to do the work required and you can't make me."

answer's not in here," locate it on your own, close the book, and hand it back, saying, "Yes it is—find it."

■ It is acceptable—and preferable—to review your child's answers and point out incorrect ones for them to correct. Again, do not give your child the correct answer.

■ If you have questions about the assignment, or your child's description of the assignment, e-mail or send a note to the teacher. Once the child realizes that you are actively going to check up on the assignment, discrepancies between what is assigned and your child's version often mysteriously disappear.

If the parents do not speak English, foreign language versions of most textbooks are available. Have your school acquire some copies, and sign them out to parents who are interested in following along with their child's progress with a textbook that they can read.

Schoolwide Assistance

Schools can establish parent centers on campus, usually in a vacant classroom. These centers are especially important in low-income, immigrant neighborhoods. They can offer parents classes in areas parallel to the student's curricula, in addition to providing assistance in various parenting areas.

For the Parent

Establish Successful Studying at Home   It is incumbent upon parents to ensure that their child has the best studying situation possible at home. This involves providing them a quiet place, the motivation required, and a workable schedule to allow them to study.

■ **Establish a study place.** You need to establish where your child will be studying. It should be somewhere quiet without distractions. If it is in the child's room, a desk should be available (preferably cleaned off so there is reasonable space on which to work). Television, stereos, iPods, and so on should be off or unavailable.

It is equally important that young siblings are controlled during this time. If this is impossible due to space considerations, try to locate an alternative place for your child to study, whether within the house, at a local public library, or possibly in a quiet room at school after the school day is over.

■ **Motivate your child.** As suggested in the previous chapter, a "No television on school nights" rule is extremely effective. Students can videotape or DVR their favorite shows during the week and watch them on the weekend.

If you tell your child that she can watch television after she is done with her homework, she *will* finish her homework more quickly. Unfortunately, it might be incomplete, incorrect, or simply below her normal ability level. If there is no motivation to watch television, then she can take her time and do the work correctly, move ahead when she is done, or maybe even read a book! This policy also should apply to video and computer games, online chatting, and other diversions.

An adaptation to this would be to allow a set, fixed time for these activities; for example, every night between seven and eight o'clock. This time limit is fixed and non-negotiable, regardless of the amount of homework or studying assigned.

■ **Provide a workable schedule.** You need to limit your child's outside activities to a reasonable level. While activities such as sports, dance, music, jobs, and so on are important and beneficial, having a two- to three-hour practice or other activity every afternoon or evening (as is often the case with "busy" children) will eventually become detrimental to the schoolwork. Given a choice, your child will always put these fun activities before homework or studying—often with your encouragement, especially if money or prestige is involved. It is up to you to place reasonable limits on your child's outside time so as to allow the child time to succeed in school.

In addition, write down progress report and report card times on your calendar. Know that the two to three weeks before these dates are usually the heaviest for homework, and try to make allowances for additional study and work time.

Support Your Child's Academic Work

■ **Talk about school.** The most important thing that you can do is demonstrate to your child that you support her work. Talk to your child every day about school. With middle or high school students, you may discover that you need to put in extra effort to extract relevant information. Note the following actual example:

Parent: What did you do in school today?

Teen: Nothing.

Parent: What happened in English class?

Teen: Nothing.

Parent: What did Ms._____ discuss today?

Teen: We went over our novel.

Parent: What did she have you do?

Teen: We had to find the theme.

Parent: What did you come up with?

Teen: Something about making choices.

Parent: What about making choices?

Teen: That good choices get you good things, bad choices get you bad things.

Parent: Give me an example.

Teen: C'mon, Mom, this is boring stuff.

Parent: No—I'm interested.

Teen: OK . . . there was this guy who . . .

It may take some work—your child may protest, delay, or try to escape from the conversation, but forcing the conversation is one of the best ways to show your child that you support what she is learning.

▪ **Establish both positive and negative consequences.** Too often, children are punished only when they perform poorly as reflected on the report card. Or they get rewarded for doing work that they are fully capable of accomplishing with little extra effort. Both are damaging to the child in the long run.

Accepting the consequences for one's work innately prepares the child for life in the adult working community. Think about it: If an adult performs poorly at a job, he is fired or demoted. If an adult performs above and beyond what is expected, a reward—raise or promotion—is often given. If the adult simply performs at the level expected, he continues at that level. Therefore, how you handle your child's school performance can directly prepare him for success in the workplace as an adult.

One way to instill this adult work ethic is to establish a contract with your child for the school year. Talk with your child to determine reasonable positive and negative consequences for her school performance. If you are uncomfortable doing this on your own, you can use the teacher as a mediator. There are two important parts to this contract: the consequences must be reasonable (positive and negative), and all parties, including the child, must agree to all portions. The consequences must be something the child greatly wants (positive) and greatly wants to avoid (negative). If the child does not agree to the contract, she will not put forth the effort to fulfill the requirements.

Here's an actual example:

The parents and the child agreed that he is capable of earning a *B* in all four of his core subjects (English, math, history, and science). When asked, the child stated that he wanted new video games as a reward. The parents agreed and the following contract for each of the four core subjects was established. For each of the ten-week grading period report cards, the following would go into effect:

- A = He gets one new game for performing above and beyond.
- B = He gets nothing; he performed at the level expected.
- C = He loses one of his games for performing less than expected.
- D = He loses two of his games for performing very poorly.
- F = Not acceptable at all; he loses entire system regardless of other grades.

The next report card, he earns one *A*, one *B*, and two *C*s. As a result, he loses one of his current favorite video games (+1, 0, −2 = −1). The next report card, he figures out he needs to work at the level required to be successful and receives three *A*s, no *B*s, and one *C*. He receives two new games (+3, 0, −1 = +2).

In this fashion, the student receives both positive and negative motivating consequences directly based on his academic performance.

Another positive consequence of the contract system is that parent nagging can be taken out of the equation. The child is directly responsible for all consequences. All the parent needs to do is say "We'll determine what happens at report card time. What you do for your grades is your choice."

Support the Academic Calendar

- **Work around the school's calendar.** The school district's calendars are usually published six to nine months in advance of the following school year. Family vacations and obligations should be planned around academic time whenever possible. (Of course, there are always exceptions, such as special family celebrations, that require an extra day or two of school time.) However, letting your child miss the first week of school, taking your child out of school the week before or after winter vacation, and things of this nature place your child at a severe disadvantage.

Absences can be a critical problem for your child in middle and high school. The first week of school, teacher-student-curriculum relationships and work requirements are established. The week before vacation often ties up the end of units (tests, projects), while the first week back starts new material. When your child is absent for an extended period (one week or more), she falls behind and can be at a disadvantage for weeks, months, and sometimes the rest of the year.

■ **Help support the standardized testing period.** In these days of the No Child Left Behind Act, testing has become critical for the school's accountability. Regardless of how wonderful your child's school is, how enriched the school's program is, or how much your child has benefited from his educational experience, if the school's standardized test scores do not increase by a certain amount every year, the school's overall program—and personnel—are in jeopardy.

These test results also directly affect your child. Entrance into advanced or gifted programs is primarily based on your child's test scores. Mandatory placement in remedial classes is almost always based on your child's test scores. The individual positive and negative consequences for your child are great; therefore, it is incumbent upon the parent to help the child succeed on these standardized tests.

There are a number of things that you as a parent can do during the two-week testing window to help your child perform as well as possible during the period. While many of these may already be part of your child's everyday routine, it is even more critical that you practice them during the school's two-week testing period:

- *Make sure your child eats a good breakfast every testing day.* Breakfast provides the energy students need to focus on the test. Hungry students cannot concentrate—that is the basis of many of the school breakfast programs around the country. Just as a football player would not think of performing in a game without eating earlier in the day, neither can students think at their peak without the nutritional energy supplied by a good breakfast.

  At the same time, you should severely limit your child's sugar intake at breakfast. A small amount of sugar is acceptable. However, the combination of sugared cereals with sugared juices and donuts or cookies is an overload. The resulting sugar high your child feels is normally followed by an even more extreme sugar low, which would most likely hit during the midmorning testing session.

- *Have your child get a good night's sleep the night before a testing day.* Sleep is as important a factor as a good breakfast. Although your child might think otherwise, insist that she get a good night's sleep in order to be fully cognizant for the next day's testing. Especially in secondary schools, many of the students do not fully wake up until second or third period. During testing days, that could cause them to do poorly on half of the test, since testing times are normally set for the first thing in the morning.

- *Get your child to school on time.* Occasionally parents run late when driving their children to school. It is critical that tardies are kept to a minimum during the testing period. Not only does being tardy stress your child, but students who arrive after the beginning of a test are not allowed to simply join in and catch up. They typically must go to a separate room to wait out the period and then take a makeup exam at a later date. This not only takes the student out of the normal testing environment but causes her to miss classes for makeup testing.

- *Try to limit your child's stress in the morning.* Although this may at times be difficult, try to limit confrontations such as arguments or punishments that could stress your child in the morning. Stressed students will not have their mind on the test at hand. Rather, they will be occupied with concentrating on what happened at home that morning. If at all possible, wait until after school or that evening to discuss problems that transpired the morning of testing.

- *Provide your child with incentives.* Just as the school undertakes motivational programs to get students to try their best on standardized tests, parents can also provide some sort of daily or weekly reward or treat if their child cooperates with the items noted above: eating a good breakfast, getting a good night's sleep, and getting out of the house on time.

(Mandel 2006a)

- **Help the school politically**. If you feel that your school is not getting the state funding you feel is appropriate, if you disagree with federal mandates imposed on your school, if you feel strongly about other political issues that affect your child's education, write, call, or e-mail your government representatives. This is one of the most effective ways of supporting the overall school program.

  Elected officials listen to parents—their constituents—much quicker than they do school personnel. If you are not sure who your government representatives are, you can go to the Web site Project Vote Smart (www.vote-smart.org/index.htm), type in your zip code, and receive information about your representatives' positions and how to contact them.

Parent Tip
Learning How Your Child Thinks

Learn how your child thinks best. There is a type of brain research entitled the multiple intelligences that studies how people think and how their brains are activated. Your child's teacher may already have this information through giving a simple multiple intelligences test. You can also discover how your child thinks best by considering the following:

■ If your child enjoys reading and writing, then he probably has a high Verbal/Linguistic Intelligence.

■ If your child enjoys logical Quest-type video games or number games, then she probably has a high Logical/Mathematical Intelligence.

■ If your child enjoys art activities, then he probably has a high Visual/Spatial Intelligence.

■ If your child enjoys sports, drama, or dancing, then she probably has a high Bodily/Kinesthetic Intelligence.

■ If your child enjoys playing an instrument or singing, then he probably has a high Musical/Rhythmic Intelligence.

■ If your child enjoys socializing or working with others, then she probably has a high Interpersonal Intelligence.

■ If your child enjoys keeping a journal or writing personal poetry, then he probably has a high Intrapersonal Intelligence.

■ If your child enjoys taking care of animals or camping, then she probably has a high Naturalist Intelligence.

By knowing what best activates your child's thinking, you can use this knowledge in helping your child study more efficiently.

If your child has a high . . .	You can help the child's thinking by . . .
Verbal/Linguistic Intelligence	Having your child explain what is being learned or discussing the material.
Logical/Mathematical Intelligence	Having your child diagram the main ideas or create some sort of flow chart that shows the logic of the ideas.
Visual/Spatial Intelligence	Having your child draw out some sort of picture explaining the material and then describing it.
Bodily/Kinesthetic Intelligence	Having your child explain the material or discussing it while going with you for a walk or some other physical activity.
Musical/Rhythmic Intelligence	Having your child explain the material or discussing it while quiet music is playing in the background.
Interpersonal Intelligence	Having your child work with a friend on the material.
Intrapersonal Intelligence	Having your child work alone or asking introspective questions such as "How would you feel . . ." or "What would you do . . ."
Naturalist Intelligence	Having your child explain the material or discussing it while sitting outside or playing with a pet.

If you would like to learn more about the multiple intelligences and how you can use them to help your child, refer to the following resources:

Armstrong, T. (2000). *Multiple Intelligences in the Classroom.* (Second Edition). Alexandria, VA: Association for Supervision and Curriculum Development.

Mandel, S. (2003). *Cooperative Work Groups: Preparing Students for the Real World.* Tucson, AZ: Corwin Press.

3

Student Learning

Mrs. Storch was frustrated. Alex was having difficulty learning his math concepts. Unfortunately, with thirty-five students in the room, it was virtually impossible for her to give him the personalized help that he needed during class. After school was not an option for additional tutoring since he needed to leave school immediately to catch a bus to get home. As with many middle school boys, he refused to take the initiative to learn the material at home. Mrs. Storch didn't know what to do to help him understand the material better so that he would succeed in her class.

Mrs. Deitch was frustrated. Her son Alex was having difficulty in his math class. She didn't know how to help him, other than to tell him to sit down and do his work. He was falling behind, spending hours on his math, and with homework for his other school subjects, their family time was decreasing by the week, having a negative impact on the entire household. She wanted to help him and she wanted him to do well, but she also wanted her family to spend their normal time together and not just wait for Alex to finish. How would she solve her dilemma?

The Issue

Student achievement is directly tied to student learning. While student learning is primarily the student's responsibility, both teachers and parents need to form a partnership in order to support and encourage the process. Remember, the vast majority of the child's awake time is spent at home, not at the school. The primary supervisor of the child's learning is therefore the parent—not the teacher. If a positive partnership does not exist between the teacher and the parent, student learning will not be as successful or as efficient as it should or could be.

Much of the material concerning student learning has already been covered in the two previous chapters. This chapter will primarily concentrate on how the curricular material itself can be shared between the school and the home, between the teacher and the parents, so that student learning occurs throughout the week and is not just confined to the student's school hours.

This particular chapter divides the overall concept of student learning into two major sections depending on the audience: For the Teacher, and For the Parent. The teacher section deals with three teacher-initiated issues: sharing information, making homework interactive, and providing parent education. The parent section concentrates on parent initiatives: interacting with the student, and interacting with the curriculum. As with all other chapters in this book, both sides of the partnership should read over and share the information with each other, so that both are aware of all issues involved with how to improve student learning.

For the Teacher

Share Information   Parents cannot assist with the curriculum, and ultimately student learning, if they do not know the curriculum. Parents must have an element of familiarity with the material in order to supervise the student's learning at home. This does not mean that you should send home your lesson plans or that the parents need to have specific knowledge of every aspect of the lessons. Rather, they should have an idea of what is expected of their child for the long term and the short term.

- **Long-term expectations.** The parents should have a copy of the state educational standards that you are following. With the standards in hand at home, they can follow along and question their child as he or she goes through your curricular material. It also becomes easier for you to send home information such as "This week we are working on history standards 4.3 and 4.6." The parents can refer to the standards and supervise their child to make sure that the child is working on the right material at home.

   Sending parents a basic syllabus at the beginning of the year can also be helpful. It does not have to be a detailed syllabus, just the basic order of topics and approximate months they will be covered. (Include the words "subject to change" to avoid any later misunderstandings.) Once again, this allows parents to keep track of their child's work.

- **Short-term expectations.** A weekly newsletter is extremely helpful in keeping parents informed of your curriculum. With a weekly newsletter, you can let them know exactly what is expected from their child that week. Individual assignments and/or topics of study can be included, allowing parents to easily keep up with their child's work and ensure that homework and class work have been completed.

A weekly newsletter does not have to be very time-consuming to prepare. It can be as basic as a one-page standardized form, with handwritten information, such as this:

> WEEK: March 4–8
>
> LANGUAGE ARTS: Finish reading Julie story. Questions 1–6, due Thursday. Spelling assignment and test due Friday.
>
> MATH: Multiplication and division of fractions. Page 46, even, due Tuesday. Page 47, #1–10, due Wednesday. Page 48, all, due Thursday. Quiz on Friday.

Detailed rubrics should also be sent to parents for all major projects. They should be signed by a parent and returned so you know that the parent read it and is aware of your requirements. When parents have the rubrics, they can better supervise their child's project to ensure that their child is following the requirements. Having rubrics also allows parents to monitor the project so that the requirements for a particular grade are completed.

Non-English-speaking parents Some of your students' parents may not speak English or may have limited English language skills. It is important that you provide these parents with the same information and curricular materials as you do for English-speaking parents. Too often the reason immigrant parents do not get involved with the curriculum is because they are embarrassed at their lack of English ability—not because they do not care, as is often assumed. Therefore, it is important for the teacher to reach out to these parents whenever possible. There are a number of ways to do this, depending on your particular classroom situation and the time you have available.

The easiest way is to provide materials in the parents' language. For general material, such as state standards and student texts, this may be fairly simple. Many of the states' standards are available online in different languages. Textbooks often have foreign language versions that can be checked out to parents. (Your school should purchase a number of these books for parental support.) If you are bilingual, or have a bilingual aide, obviously material can be translated. Although this will take additional time, it will be worth it in the long run—especially if some of your materials (such as project rubrics) can be saved from year to year.

There are other less common but valuable ways to get curricular informational material to non-English-speaking parents. One easy way is to incorporate a buddy system. If you have a small number of non-English-speaking parents in your class, you can ask a couple of parents who are bilingual to volunteer as buddies. Whenever you send home parent material, the buddy automatically calls the non-English-speaking parent and translates the material over the phone. If that parent has questions or concerns, those are relayed to you via the bilingual parent. I have found that parents are more than wiling to serve as bilingual buddies. As a result, the non-English-speaking parents become less embarrassed about contacting the teacher and more involved in their child's education.

Another way that you can directly translate material into every major language is through the use of the Web site Alta Vista Babel Fish Translation (www.babelfish.altavista.com). On this site, you cut and paste your newsletter, or portions of your parent information, into their "translation box." With one click, the site translates the information for you. You then cut and paste the translated text into a word processing document and print it out for your non-English-speaking parents. It is really that simple—it takes less than a minute to cut, paste, translate, cut, and paste text back into a document. The site also works with entire Web pages. With just a few extra minutes of effort, you can have all of your home curricular information translated, giving all of your parents access to the material and enabling them to assist their child with his student learning.

Make Homework Interactive   Probably the easiest way to get parents directly involved in student learning is to make homework and projects interactive. This does not mean creating parent sections of homework. Rather, this means the parents and their child working together to learn together, with the parent supporting the student learning. "Involvement" does not mean simply overseeing the student's curricular material. Involvement means active participation, which is important in demonstrating to the child that the parent is interested and, more important, a full partner in student learning.

The parent interactive component can be direct, working with the actual classroom curricula, or supplemental, expanding student knowledge in the various curricular areas.

- **Direct involvement.** Teachers can include parents in their assignments in a variety of ways. Student questions or activities can be included that have to be discussed with the parent. For example, in a math unit on percentages, the student can work with parents on how to figure out percentages of family income that go to various categories such as housing or food. Or they can take a trip to the mall, look at a sales rack, and determine percentages of markdowns and before and/or after costs. In a literature unit, you can have the student read specific chapters to the parents and have the parents react to and discuss the material based on questions that you send home.

  As you develop this material, keep in mind that parents probably have very little experience with the concept of higher order critical thinking questions. You can send questions home for parents to use in discussing the material with their child. As the parents work with the questions, they gradually learn about higher order critical thinking strategies, thereby increasing the level of their involvement. This can be especially effective when their child is studying for a unit or chapter exam. For example, here are some questions based on Bloom's *Taxonomy* (Bloom 1953) that can be sent home for a final study session for a unit on the Civil War:

  - *Knowledge:* Who was the general who finally led the North to victory?
  - *Understanding:* What was the single event that ultimately caused the South to secede from the Union?

- *Application:* What did the Southern states have in common that caused them to band together?
- *Analysis:* What advantages and disadvantages did the North and the South each have?
- *Synthesis:* Why did the North ultimately win the war? Name at least three reasons.
- *Evaluation:* Pretend that one of you is a farmer in Massachusetts and the other is a farmer in South Carolina. Make arguments for your side in the Civil War. Why were you justified in going to war?

You can include answers for the parent, or not. Having the student explain and prove her answer, using notes or the text, should be enough for the home discussion.

Another way to get parents directly involved is to send home tutoring work every month for their child. Granted, this involves a considerable amount of additional work and is probably more applicable to a limited roster of students such as elementary classes or secondary special education. The tutoring packets that you send home should be highly individualized and focus on that student's particular deficiencies. Include tips for parents on how to work with the child at home. (These tips can be general ones— working on multiplication facts, working on spelling words—that could be regularly duplicated to ultimately reduce the workload required for this activity.)

- **Supplemental involvement.** One of the easiest and most enjoyable ways to promote student learning is when parents supplement the curriculum at home. Field trips to local museums are a great family activity for a weekend. You need to stay current on what is available in your community and send home information for the parent for each curricular unit. This can be a valuable addition to your students' curriculum as it will assist with experiential activities for which you do not have time or budget within the school day.

The following are a variety of home supplemental activities that you can suggest to the parent which would add to the curricula:

- *English:* Rent the movie for a work of literature that you are reading in class. Have the student compare and contrast the movie with the book.
- *Math:* Take a trip to the mall and graph the percentages of shoe stores, food stores, etc.
- *History:* Take a trip to the local museums to see a special exhibit based on the area you are studying. Provide the parents with guiding questions.
- *Science:* Take a trip to a local science museum or zoological park focusing on a specific area being studied. Provide the parents with guiding questions.

One of the best, and newest, types of supplemental involvement for parents is the use of virtual field trips. Virtual field trips are online sensory experiences that parents and students can share together. They can be as simple as a list of Web sites to visit or as complicated as a fully developed virtual field trip sent home on a CD-ROM. (See *Cybertrips in Social Studies*, Mandel 2002, for a full discussion of how to create simple virtual field trips.) The following is an example of a section of a simple virtual field trip to the culture of Shakespeare's time. This virtual field trip was given to the parents in the form of a two-page itinerary, which the parents and student could follow step-by-step. The layout was very simple:

1. A one- or two-sentence explanation of what was to be visited at that site
2. The title of the site
3. The site's URL
4. Any additional information, if needed, as to how to navigate the site to locate the information

The virtual field trip was typed into a word-processing document, then duplicated for each family:

Start your trip with a virtual tour of the Globe Theater, where Shakespeare performed his works:

Shakespeare's Globe Theater—Virtual Tour

www.shakespeares-globe.org (Click on "Exhibition" on top, "Theater Tours" on the left side, then "Virtual Tour" on the bottom of the page.)

Take a look at the clothing of Shakespeare's time:

The Middle Ages—Clothing

www.learner.org/exhibits/middleages/clothing.html

Life in a medieval village was quite different than life in cities today. Take a tour of the medieval village of Wichamstow:

The Village of Wichamstow

www.regia.org/village.htm

Providing Parent Education　Many parents want to assist their child with curricular work but simply do not know enough about the material. The teacher can be a critical resource in providing parent education so that parents are informed enough about the subject matter to fully participate in the student's learning.

■ **Curricular parent workshops.** Parent workshops can provide information on topics at an adult level. It is important not to simply present the students' curriculum as you would teach it to your class. That can easily be considered condescending and is an immediate turnoff to the parents. Present the same material, but on their level of sophistication. For example, sessions featuring a movie and discussion of a piece of literature read by the students, or a discussion of a period of history using the Internet and a projector, can present the student's basic curriculum to the parents on an adult level.

■ **Special curricular events.** Special curricular events that students and their parents attend together, such as a math, science, or reading night, are wonderful ways to involve parents in student learning. Family curricular games can be played or activities and presentations shared. The value of these events is that parents experientially learn how to interact with the subject matter and how to better relate to the student's work at home.

Teacher-directed family field trips are another way to involve parents experientially with the material. These differ from those proposed in the previous section in that they are led by the teacher. You can arrange to meet with interested families at a museum or community activity on the weekend and guide them through the experience, having greater control over what is being taught or experienced.

■ **Curricular visitations.** Parents who are really interested in getting involved with student learning should be invited to sit in on the classroom lessons. In this situation, the parents act like a student teacher who is observing a veteran teacher. By observing the teacher teach a lesson, parents better learn how the student is being taught and can replicate or supplement the material more efficiently at home.

For lower-income populations, the school can consider funding the opening of the school computer lab two or three nights a week. With this opportunity, parents who cannot afford home computers or online services can still fully participate in technological aspects of the curriculum, such as virtual field trips.

For the Parent

Interacting with the Student   Direct interaction with your child is the most basic way to get involved with student learning, regardless of any familiarity with the actual curricula.

■ **Talk to your child.** Every day, ask your child to name one thing that he learned in school that day. This may take a little prodding, especially with teenagers.

When questioning your child, timing is important for your success in eliciting information. One of the worst times to ask these questions is in the car on the way home from school (especially if your child's peers are in attendance). Your child is most likely "wired" from the school day and needs some mental relaxation after school. Later in the evening, when your child is more relaxed, is a much better time to get information about the school day.

When asking your child about the day, be sure to ask probing questions, not just "What did you learn today?" Some examples are:

■ What was the main topic your teacher talked about?
■ What was written on the board for the class agenda today?
■ What was the most important idea that your teacher wanted you to learn today?

You can also have some fun and get creative with your questioning by using the following prompts:

■ Give me a newspaper headline for your lesson today.
■ It's *Jeopardy* time—give me a fact that you learned in class and I'll try to get the question correct.

■ **Make time to study with your child.** Spend some time actually learning the material with your child. If you do not understand some aspect of the curricula, have your child "teach" it to you. Not only will you learn the material, but your child will actually understand it much better as she has to use higher order critical thinking skills to synthesize the material to teach it to you.

■ **Go through your child's backpack.** Regularly go through your child's backpack to see what he is doing and what you are missing. Be sure, however, that your child is present—it is a matter of respect of the child's privacy. By going through the backpack, you may discover class work, tests, assignments, and other materials that may not have made their way to you.

■ **Oversee assignments.** Please keep in mind that your child spends much more of his week outside of the classroom than within. An even greater percentage of individualized work time is conducted at home rather than at school. Therefore, you are your child's primary schoolwork supervisor.

Create or purchase a large wall calendar and post it in your child's room. As assignments are given, make sure that they are written on the calendar. Pay close attention to due dates and other benchmark periods for long-term assignments or large projects. Once this information is posted, work with your child to plan out her work progress throughout the assignments, monitoring that she does not fall behind. It is important that your child do the actual planning—with your supervision—so that personal responsibility is developed.

■ **Provide a good study environment.** Probably one of the greatest ways you can assist your child is to ensure he has a good study environment. As discussed in full in chapter 2, the keys to creating a good study environment are:

  ■ Establish a quiet, set place to study with a desk.
  ■ Eliminate distractions (TVs, music, and so on).
  ■ Limit disturbances from siblings.

Interacting with the Curriculum   Interaction with the curriculum refers to the ways parents can acquire curricular information on their own in order to help them raise the level of student learning. This information may be on an adult level, as a form of personal learning of the subject matter, or it may be on the student's level, as a way to provide additional assistance when the student is experiencing difficulty with a concept.

By learning, or becoming familiar with, the same basic subjects as your child, you can assist her when she is having problems or be better able to supervise her work since you are familiar with the actual curricular material being studied.

- **Know the state curricular standards.** All school curricula today is standards-based. Textbooks and curricula must follow specific state educational standards,. Your school should be able to provide you with a copy of these standards so you can follow along with the specific standards your child's teacher is covering.

  If the school cannot provide you with the state's educational standards, you can locate them online at the Education World: State Standards Web site, www.education-world.com/standards/state/index.shtml. Simply select your state from the pull-down menu and get links to every educational standard from that state.

  As you work with the state standards, be aware that they are often no more than general areas of information to be learned. Every teacher and every textbook varies in the presentation of the material, and very often the actual order in which it is presented. However, if your child is on a specific unit, chances are good that the state standards will provide you with an overview of what your child should be learning.

- **Using the Internet to find curricular material.** The Internet is the ultimate educational resource center. You can use online resources to locate almost any educational material you desire. Whether you want to educate yourself on a subject or locate supplemental material for your child, the Internet is a critical resource.

Parent Tip

What If the Web Site URL Doesn't Work? Don't Panic!

Some of the Web site URLs that you receive from your child's teacher, this book, or other sources may not work when you try them. That is simply the nature of the Internet—it is fluid and constantly changing.

Don't panic if you type in a URL and it does not work.

Follow these steps to correct the problem:

1. Double-check that every symbol you typed in the URL is correct—periods, underscores, symbols, etc. The slightest mistake in typing will cause the site not to connect.

2. Take the exact title of the site and search for it through Google (www.google.com). Very often sites change their URLs, and the one you are given will no longer work, even though the site still exists.

3. Use the sites listed in this chapter—the general education and the subject matter sites—and search for a new site with similar material. There are hundreds of educational Internet sites with duplicate subject matter! If the one you have no longer works, find another. (However, don't do a Google search for these. Chances are you will not be provided with good *educational* sites.)

The following are excellent educational Web sites that you can refer to for curricular material. Bookmark them on your computer, or keep this list available for future reference.

Virtually any educational source can be located using the general education Internet site called Teachers Helping Teachers (www.pacificnet.net/~mandel). Click on the link to Educational Resources and then scroll down through the following sections: Arts, Early Childhood/ Primary Grades, Elective Courses, Language Arts, History/Social Studies, Math, Multicultural, Science, Social Action, Special Education/Gifted, Teacher Resources.

The links listed on this site are general, but each one contains hundreds of links of its own. Therefore, you can use this site as a portal to get any online information you want, simply by moving from general topics to specific ones.

The following list includes subject matter sites that you can use for more specific subject matter material, along with a couple of resource sites. All of these can be used to increase your personal knowledge or help you with your child's curricular material:

Curricular-Specific Sites

Language Arts

Children's Literature Web Guide

www.ucalgary.ca/~dkbrown/index.html

■ Pay special attention to the "More Links" section.

Math

AAA Math

www.aaamath.com

■ Select from topics or grade levels for information and games.

History/Social Studies

History/Social Studies Web Site for K-12 Teachers

http://k-12historysocialstudies.com/boals.html

■ Pay special attention to the various history links in the third row.

Science

Cody's Science Education Zone

http://tlc.ousd.k12.ca.us/~acody

■ Select the "Links" button on the left for all types of science sites.

Resource Sites

Gifted Education

Hoagies' Gifted Education Page

www.hoagiesgifted.org

■ Pay special attention to the "Parents" link.

Creating Educational Puzzles and Games for Your Child

Puzzlemaker

http://puzzlemaker.school.discovery.com

■ Select from the "Create Puzzles Online" section.

A Safe Search Engine for Kids Created by Librarians

Kidsclick

http://kidsclick.org

■ Use it as a safe, regular search engine; select from the categories or search words.

Reference Center—Libraries, Books, and More

Library Spot

www.libraryspot.com

■ Select from the list of resources on the left side.

■ **Use the teacher as a resource.** Your child's teacher is probably the greatest resource for obtaining curricular material. He or she will gladly answer your questions or direct you to the best place to locate the information.

If you are really interested in learning exactly how the material is being taught so as to duplicate the process at home, ask your child's teacher if you could attend a couple of lessons. By observing the teacher, you can get a good feel for how the subject matter is being taught. However, please be flexible and understanding. Let the teacher know what you are interested in learning, and then he can invite you in at the most appropriate time.

4

Volunteering

Ms. Phillips was frustrated. This year she had a number of parents who were accustomed to volunteering in their children's classroom in elementary school. Unfortunately, even though their children had entered middle school, the parents still wanted to be in the classroom to help. It wasn't that she was worried that they were there to "watch her." The majority of them truly enjoyed assisting their child's teacher. The problem was that she had little for them to do. She ran a very self-sufficient program and had no need for parent volunteers. She didn't even utilize the student aides that were available in the school. Eventually, the parents felt insulted that their help was not needed. Ms. Phillips tried to figure out how she could get her parents involved as volunteers while still maintaining her set classroom program.

Ms. Gonzalez was frustrated. She regularly volunteered in her daughter's classroom all through the child's elementary school years. Now that her child was in middle school, the teachers did not seem to want her around. She wanted to help and offered her assistance a number of times to each one of her daughter's six teachers, but not one of them accepted it (other than to have her tag along as a field trip chaperone). She grew increasingly insulted and slowly began to wonder what the teachers were trying to hide from the parents. Ms. Gonzalez wanted to know how she could volunteer in her daughter's school, even if the teachers didn't want the help in the individual classrooms.

The Issue

Other than attending school functions such as open house, shows, or concerts, parent volunteering has been the primary way parents have been involved in the school program. Parent volunteering is a critical element in any school, elementary, middle, or high. As the National Parent Teacher Association (PTA) has described:

> Literally millions of dollars of volunteer services are performed by parents and family members each year in the public schools. Studies have concluded that volunteers express greater confidence in the schools where they have opportunities to participate regularly. In addition, assisting in school or program events/activities communicates to a child, "I care about what you do here."

> (National PTA 1998)

Unfortunately, parent volunteering in the classroom is usually limited to the elementary grades. Parent volunteering in the school is usually limited to PTA or booster club activities and fundraisers, or as chaperones on field trips. And families with two working parents rarely get to participate in school volunteer work. This current situation is not an example of a true teacher-parent partnership.

Teachers do not have enough time to do everything they want in the classroom. Schools do not have enough funding to do everything they want for the educational program. Parent volunteers can assist with both of these problems, and at the same time lend their time and strengths to the school environment. From the university-educated professional to the stay-at-home parent with a high school education, all parents have a tremendous amount of resources to share. Therefore, it is up to both the teacher and the parent to discover the best way to utilize their talents while taking into account the desires of both sides. This is not an easy task, but it is an important one.

A positive and productive attitude on both sides—teacher and parent—is critical to a successful volunteer program.

Teachers need to consider the parent as a valuable resource to employ whenever possible. They need to consider nontraditional ways to get parents involved beyond simple tasks in the classroom and chaperoning on field trips. Teachers also must realize that the majority of parents are not the enemy—they are not in the classroom to spy or acquire special treatment for their child. They are there to help, and it is up to the teacher to figure out how the parents can help.

At the same time, parents need to ask themselves why they want to volunteer—what is their agenda? Do they want to better the school program or are they only interested in their own child's experience? The two reasons are very different. In the former, the parent is interested in doing whatever the school or teacher asks him to do, assisting wherever needed based on his talents and resources. This leads to cooperation. In the latter, the parent decides how to get involved— regardless of the teacher's needs or desires. This inevitably leads to conflict. In the first instance, the parent works for the school. In the second, the school works for the parent. It is a critical distinction, and one that must be addressed for a successful parent volunteer program.

Ways to Involve Parents as Volunteers

There are many ways to involve parents as volunteers outside of the traditional ones (PTA activities and field trip chaperones). The following list includes ten types of nontraditional activities and services parents can provide to enhance the students' educational program. This particular section is designed for both teachers and parents, so that one party can suggest these roles to the other throughout the school year. The activities are further categorized in two ways:

- **Long-term versus short-term:** Long-term activities are those that go on throughout the year, or at least over the course of a few months. They require the most substantial commitment from the parent. Short-term activities may last for a day or two, and involve much less of a time commitment.

- **School versus home:** Most parent volunteer activities must be conducted at the school. This can be very difficult for parents who work full-time outside of the house. However, a number of these activities can be performed at home so that parents who can't spend significant time at the school can still volunteer in their child's educational program.

For the Teacher and the Parents:

- **Tutoring (long-term/school).** Tutoring can be provided by parents as a way of assisting students who are either below grade level or having difficulty with a higher-level course. For example, parents can help elementary students with their reading skills or learning their multiplication facts. Parents can also assist middle or high school students with algebra (assuming that they are familiar with the subject). Parent tutoring can be conducted at a set time every week during class, or as an after-school program.

    This tutorial work does not have to be limited to sitting with individual students. Parent volunteers can conduct reading circles in elementary classes, taking the role of a classroom aide or paraprofessional. They can assist a group of students in studying for an exam in any subject, asking them questions or playing a curricular review type of game.

In any of these formats, a parent volunteer is acting as an educational aide in the instructional program of the classroom, under the direction of the teacher.

■ **Mentoring at-risk students (long-term/school).** Very often at-risk students (those in serious danger of dropping out in the future) need mentors to help them. This mostly affects middle and high school students. A caring adult is often all a troubled student needs to turn around, try harder, and ultimately stay in school and out of trouble.

When you mentor an at-risk student, you periodically visit her throughout the school year (usually at least once a week). You check on her attendance, help her with academic subjects in which she may be having trouble, and basically listen. You are there as a friend and caring adult. If serious issues arise that you feel must be addressed by someone with professional counseling training, you can refer the student to a school counselor or a specialized school program dealing with at-risk students.

■ **Replacing cut programs (long-term/school).** Over the past decade, educational budgets all over the country have been slashed. As a direct result, many extra programs—especially in the arts—have been cut from the school day. Parents who have expertise in these specialized areas can volunteer their time to teach these classes during the day in elementary school, or after school in secondary programs. Instrumental or vocal music, art, dance, drama, ceramics, and home economics are just some of the extra programs that have been eliminated but can be reestablished through the use of parent volunteers. This is an easy way to enrich the overall school educational program during times of budgetary restraints.

■ **Extracurricular programs (long-term/school).** Not only have supplemental programs been eliminated within the school day, but numerous after-school extracurricular activities have also been cut from the schools, especially at the elementary and middle school levels. Students—especially middle school students—need supervision after school and extracurricular activities are an excellent way to provide it. Parent volunteers can run after-school programs in various subjects such as the arts, sports, drill team, science clubs, and more.

Check with your local school district to see if there are organizations that oversee extracurricular programs of this type. If so, parents can apply to teach some of these classes every week. If there is no formal organization, the school itself can offer these sessions as a way of enriching the students' day. The commitment can vary—the classes can be offered for the entire year, a semester, or a shorter period such as four, six, or eight weeks.

■ **Clerical help (short-term/school).** Offering clerical help to teachers can help them get through some of the paperwork that increasingly affects teachers' time. This assistance can include not only paperwork within the classroom but also things such as duplicating papers and other busy work. Ultimately, volunteer help with clerical work frees up the teacher for more teaching and curricular preparation. However, there are two major categories of clerical work in which parents should never be involved: grading papers and filing personal information.

Parents should never grade papers. Papers reflect private information about students—peers of the parent's child—that is inappropriate for the parent to see. The parent might share or spread this information, placing the teacher in a very uncomfortable situation. Even an incidental carpool comment to a child, such as "Mike, I saw you didn't do very well on your test," can create tensions within the classroom. The exception to this principle is when the parent volunteer does not see the student names on the papers he or she is grading. This can be accomplished by using student ID numbers instead of names or by using Scantron-type sheets.

For similar reasons, parent volunteers should never do filing work that involves student files. This includes not only the school records but also the individual teacher's classroom files. The key here is anything that contains personal information about students should be off-limits for parent volunteers.

■ **Providing help locating online curricular material (short-term/home).** This is a new area where parent volunteers can provide a significant service to the teacher, even if they work all day and are unable to come to the school. This is especially valuable if the teacher uses cooperative work groups within the classroom. Parent volunteers can use the Internet to locate curricular material for the vertical files used in the cooperative work group experience (Mandel 2003).

However, this curricular service does not have to be limited to cooperative work group experiences. Any unit for which the teacher would like to acquire new supplementary material is appropriate for this volunteer assistance.

A few weeks before the introduction of any new unit, the teacher should send home a letter asking parents to search for, and send in, material in specific topic areas. For example, a month before a unit on the solar system is to commence, the following letter is sent to parents who had previously offered to help with this process:

Thank you for helping locate new supplemental material for our science curriculum! We are about to begin a unit on the solar system. Please go online and locate and print out interesting material in the following areas:

Space bodies—planets, moon, asteroids, comets

Stars and constellations

The Hubble telescope

Other new space discoveries

Please send in the material you locate with your child no later than _____.

Once this material is collected, the teacher analyzes the contributions and selects those most appropriate for integration into the curriculum. A great many teacher hours spent searching for the latest online curricular material can be averted by having parent volunteers do the basic legwork. In addition, this is a great opportunity for parents who work to add to the school's curricular program. (Please note, this is one area where you want to send letters home *only* to those parents who had previously expressed a desire to help, rather than to everybody. Those without Internet access at home may feel offended or inadequate because they cannot afford this technology and therefore cannot help as other parents can.)

■ **Creating/maintaining a classroom Web site (long-term/home).** Another way that parent volunteers can help with online resources is by creating or maintaining a classroom Web site. Very often teachers want to establish a classroom Web site but do not have the knowledge or the time to do so. A parent knowledgeable in Web site development can create and operate the site for the teacher.

The teacher simply needs to determine what material she wants to include on the Web site. She can type it into a word processing document and send it home to the parent volunteer, or she can e-mail the information. The parent takes the teacher's material and creates the actual site. Updates to the information are supplied by the teacher throughout the year on a weekly or a monthly basis. In this fashion, all of the material for the classroom Web site is supplied by the teacher, but the time involved to create and maintain the Web site is supplied by a parent volunteer working from home.

■ **After-school supervision (long-term/school).** Schools normally have logistical difficulty in supervising all of the physical campus areas that need to be supervised after school to prevent student problems or vandalism. Areas that typically need attention include all crosswalks or carpool pick-up locations, along with the inner school grounds themselves. Due to budgetary constraints, schools simply have too many locations to supervise and not enough after-school personnel. Parent volunteers can take up a lot of this slack.

Parents can maintain some semblance of order simply by being present. By having the school issue these volunteers a special colored vest (orange or red are the most common), the supervisory volunteer is immediately noticeable. They can watch that students use crosswalks and parents do not park illegally.

As added benefits, having a noticeable adult present automatically improves student behavior, and volunteers can immediately bring problems to the school office's attention. Having parent volunteers roam the campus during the hour after school will also reduce vandalism. Please note that this does not mean that parents are to handle discipline. They are there to supervise, be noticed, and advise. By issuing these volunteers walkie-talkies, they can immediately contact the school office when a serious problem develops, thereby allowing the school personnel to quickly take care of the problem.

■ **Phone-trees (long-term/home).** Another way that parents who work all day can become volunteers is through the use of phone-trees. Normally phone-trees are used to remind parents of school events. However, these classroom phone-trees can be directly incorporated into the classroom curriculum. Reminders of dates of major tests or projects can be shared with parents through this medium, along with special information about classroom events.

To start the phone-tree, the teacher calls the parent who is chairing this activity. The teacher shares the information that needs to be distributed. That parent passes the information on to the five to eight additional parents helping him. Each of those parents is assigned to five to eight parents of their own. The message is passed along to them, and so on.

This phone-tree program is especially effective for non-English-speaking parents. They can directly receive classroom information in their native language, without requiring the teacher to take the additional time to have the material translated.

■ **Donating money or materials (short-term/home).** Sometimes the easiest way for working parents to volunteer is through donating money or materials. While this may not be considered the best way to volunteer, it does provide a valuable service to the classroom curriculum.

At the beginning of the year, or before a new unit, the teacher can send out a wish list of things that the school cannot afford. Parents can then donate money or purchase items on the list. As an extra incentive, the teacher can supply a donation letter with the school tax ID number, to be used for income tax purposes.

Some schools (usually in higher income areas) institute a "pay or play" system. They require each family to donate a certain amount of money for materials or for extracurricular activities. Parents who cannot afford to donate can choose to donate a certain amount of volunteer hours instead.

Important Factors to Consider with a Volunteer Program

To establish a positive and productive classroom volunteer program, you must consider a number of factors. You cannot simply say to parents, "Here's what I need to have done. Who wants to help?" Many parent volunteers are professionals; all of them are adults. They must be treated with respect for them to want to help—and to help in a positive manner. On the other hand, parent volunteers must remember that it is the teacher's classroom and the teacher's program, and there may be some restrictions on volunteer activities. Most important, parent volunteers need to remember that the classroom has many children, not just their own.

The following are some significant issues that teachers and parents need to consider to establish a positive, working volunteer program that incorporates the teacher-parent partnership concept. These include particular teacher issues, and issues most appropriate for the parent.

For the Teacher

- **Establishing the volunteer program.** There are two critical components to the establishment of a successful volunteer program. The first is to determine in advance the areas for which you want parent assistance throughout the year. The second is to determine the ways in which you want parent volunteers to help.

  When determining the areas for which you want volunteer help, first consider your previous experiences. Ask yourself three basic questions:

  - How have you successfully used parent volunteers in the past?
  - How have you unsuccessfully used parent volunteers in the past?
  - Looking over the ten areas listed previously, and considering your educational program, where do you think parent volunteers can assist you this year?

  The answers to these questions will determine where you incorporate parents within your classroom program.

  Now that you know where you would like assistance, you need to determine if your criteria match the volunteer interests of your parents. The easiest way to determine the areas in which parents want to help is through the use of a parent questionnaire. It is very important that you design your own questionnaire—do not use one created by the school or an outside source. Premade questionnaires may ask for interest in areas in which you do not want assistance. Parents who then state they want to assist in those areas and are subsequently not asked to do so may feel slighted and less supportive overall. Therefore, based on your personal, predetermined classroom needs, you settle on the criteria found on the questionnaire.

  Once you review the parent questionnaires, you need to determine the types of activities in which individual parents want to participate. Do they want to help with busy work? Do they want to work directly with children?

Do they want to work at home? It is critical that you do not waste a volunteer's time with something she has no desire to do. Remember: to be worthwhile, parent volunteer work needs to be meaningful and valuable to the parent. Otherwise, the volunteering will end very quickly.

Very often schools have a plethora of parent volunteers. This phenomenon allows you to examine the assistance that they can provide on a broader trans-classroom basis. You can efficiently organize this classroom assistance by establishing a schoolwide volunteer program through a Parent Volunteer Department. Headed by an administrator, teacher, or parent volunteer, this department oversees all volunteering opportunities throughout the school. In this fashion, parents who wish to volunteer can be placed in the specific areas where they are needed. Be aware, however, that this can only work if you have parents who are willing to work anywhere in the school for the betterment of the overall educational program. It won't work if your parent volunteers insist on serving only in their child's classroom.

■ **Educate the volunteers.** It is important that you treat classroom volunteers as paraprofessionals, especially when they will be working with students. They must be shown exactly what to do and how to do it; you can't just tell them something like "Work with the students on this." This may be somewhat time-consuming at the beginning, but it will create a much more productive assistance program for the long-term.

Parent volunteers who are working with students need to be shown how to tutor or work with groups. There are two important variables involved with this type of in-service work—learning teaching methodologies and learning about individual students.

Obviously, parent volunteers are not educators, and should not be given significant teaching tasks. However, there are some simple teaching methodologies that you can demonstrate to the parent volunteer through simple modeling. This is an especially important procedure if the volunteer work is to be long-term. Taking a day or two to have the parent observe you modeling how to tutor, or how to best work with a group, can go a long way toward ensuring that the parent does the task correctly later. This is particularly important with group work, where even slight nuances such as how you hold a story book, where you pause in your reading, and how you ask questions, is a teaching skill that you have perfected over the years. By modeling the correct teaching methodologies and pointing out important steps within the methodologies, you will have a better chance of turning a parent volunteer into a valuable paraprofessional.

When you have a parent volunteer working with students, especially on an individualized basis, it is important that you share certain behaviors that the student might demonstrate to an adult other than you. You, as the teacher, are aware of tricks and behaviors that students exhibit in front of an uninformed adult, such as a substitute teacher. Very often the student will treat the parent volunteer the same way when your attention is elsewhere.

For example, here are some behaviors students might exhibit that should be shared with a parent tutor:

- Constantly asking for help or for the correct answers when the student should know the material
- Being off-task more than normal
- Continually coming up with excuses for not completing or attempting certain work that the student should be able to do
- Requiring extra explanations, or explanations in a particular form, in order to complete assignments

These are just a sampling of student behaviors that a parent volunteer tutor should be aware of prior to the working session. The rule of thumb is if the student regularly attempts to get away with things in your absence, or if a particular child requires specialized assistance, then the parent tutor should always be informed of these behaviors prior to the tutoring session.

■ **Show appreciation and respect for volunteers.** Parent volunteers are donating their time and effort. Almost all of them could find other things to do with their time rather than spend hours assisting you in your work. Therefore, it is imperative that you show appreciation and respect to volunteers.

Most schools have volunteer appreciation luncheons in the spring. However, a personal touch—a card from you, lunch if the parent volunteers on a long-term basis—is appreciated even more. Having students who benefited from the volunteer program create cards or some other personalized gesture is a great avenue to pursue.

If parents volunteer and you do *not* use their services for whatever reason, call or write to them and thank them for their generous offer, and let them know why their help is not currently needed. This will help alleviate any ill will for not taking them up on their attempt to help.

Probably the greatest way that you can demonstrate your appreciation of their time is to not waste it. Do not create busy work for a parent volunteer just because she is there. If a parent shows up and you do not have anything worthwhile for her to do, explain the situation and ask whether she would mind assisting another teacher or the office personnel. If so, contact someone who you think might be able to use her help, and direct her that way.

For the Parent

■ **Sometimes individual teachers do not want volunteers.** There are many teachers who simply do not want to incorporate volunteers into their daily educational program, for one reason or another. Parents who had been very active in their child's elementary school often become frustrated when their child enters middle school, where fewer teachers use parent volunteers in the classroom. Parents need to accept this situation.

When a teacher does not want to incorporate parent volunteers into the classroom, it does not mean that the teacher has something to hide. Many teachers have very set, structured programs and specific ways of doing things, which they prefer to operate themselves. For example, a teacher may want to be the sole person grading papers, or all of the teaching time is either teacher-directed or in student-led cooperative work groups. Sometimes it just takes more time or effort to educate a parent volunteer on how to do one of the teacher's procedures than the assistance is worth. Also, a teacher may have had problems with parent volunteers in the past and concluded that it is easier to do the work herself.

If a teacher turns down a request to volunteer, the parent needs to question if the teacher is rejecting all help or, more likely, rejecting the particular type of assistance the parent is offering. This is an important distinction, especially when moving from primary grades to upper elementary to middle school. Teachers at different levels require different things. If a teacher does not take you up on your offer to read to students, it does not necessarily mean that he is rejecting you as a parent volunteer. Rather, it more than likely means that he does not need someone coming into the room to read to students. In this case you should ask if there are other services you can render during the school day or at home. (Refer to the list of volunteer suggestions.)

Teacher needs are very different at the secondary school level. Instead of having the same students for the majority of the day as in elementary school, these teachers often have to cover their curriculum in a forty-five- to fifty-minute period. There simply is limited time for elementary school–type volunteer activities.

If you discover that your child's teacher does not need your assistance, broaden your scope and see if you can help the school in some other capacity. There may be other teachers who can use your time. The school office personnel or the PTA may need an extra pair of hands. As was initially stated in this chapter, if you are there to better the school's overall program versus just working in your child's classroom, there will be numerous opportunities for you to volunteer your services, even if they are not with your child's teacher.

■ **When you should *not* be in your child's classroom.** There are times where it may actually be inappropriate to volunteer in your child's classroom. One of these situations was mentioned earlier—when the volunteer work involves knowledge of other students' grades or achievement levels. Grading papers, filing personal material, and activities of this nature are sometimes a great help. However, these activities should be pursued in a classroom where you do not know the children. This will help alleviate many confidentiality concerns.

Another time you probably should not volunteer in your child's classroom is when your child is in the fourth grade or higher. At this point, the child's social group becomes the most significant part of her life. Unfortunately, it is also at this time that students mercilessly tease each other. Having Mommy in the classroom could cause some anxiety for your child, even if you do not directly observe it.

This is not a hard-and-fast rule, however. There are times when you may be providing a special service or program for the students, such as when a parent who is an expert on Shakespeare talks to a high school English class. Sometimes a teacher needs parent volunteers to chaperone on field trips. When these options are available in secondary school, try to supervise a group that does *not* include your child, unless your child directly requests it.

There are also the "cool" parents who are socially accepted by your child's peers and can get away with more contact than others. But be aware—even these parents have their limitations, especially from eighth grade up through high school.

■ **Consistency is important for long-term volunteer work.** It is disrespectful and problematic for a parent volunteer to not show up when expected. Many curricular volunteer programs (those working with reading groups or tutoring) benefit most by having the parent volunteer come at a regular time each week. If you have established a set time, it is critical that you show up at that time on a consistent basis, because the teacher is planning on it.

The teacher normally has a set daily schedule established in advance, based on the day's curriculum, the needs of students, and the accessibility of school or volunteer services. If a parent volunteer is expected at 9:30 on Tuesday to work with a group of students, then that is planned within the day. If the parent does not show up at that time, the teacher's plans have suddenly been altered. Either those particular students do not get the assistance scheduled for that time or the teacher has to suddenly divert her attention from other teaching that was previously planned. The educational program for that day is negatively affected.

Parent volunteers must remember that if they are expected at a certain time, for a certain task, they need to show up on time. They cannot be late or absent just because they are "only" volunteering. Concern about the reliability of parent volunteers is one reason many teachers do not use volunteers for curricular assistance.

- **Trust is critical.** Unfortunately, another significant reason teachers do not use parent volunteers is because many abuse trust. This is especially true when a parent comes into a classroom with a hidden agenda. When you are in the classroom as a parent volunteer, you are there to assist the teacher, not spy on the teacher.

You also may hear or see confidential information about individual students while in the classroom. You need to be trusted to act professionally and not repeat things that you see or hear that are of a personal nature. If you break that trust, you will discover that your volunteering services will be rarely used in the future.

If you question something that you observe while working as a volunteer, talk to the teacher privately. Often you will be given an explanation as to what is occurring. Sometimes the teacher may say that the information is confidential. In that case, you must respect the teacher's answer. Speak to the school administration only if you see something that is exceedingly unprofessional. Issues such as a disagreement with how the teacher teaches or manages a classroom should be left with the teacher. A parent volunteer is there to assist the teacher, not report on the teacher.

Remember that teachers are human. A teacher's patience level at two o'clock on Thursday afternoon may be different than it is at ten o'clock Tuesday morning. The same student behaviors that are acceptable in October may be totally inappropriate in May.

For example, if you observe the teacher doing something with which you disagree, such as raising his voice to a student, do not simply get upset and complain that the teacher was "yelling at students." Talk to the teacher about your concerns and find out the details and context of the situation. It may be that that particular student had been in trouble six times already that day, and by the seventh occurrence the teacher had run out of normal patience.

Parents find themselves in this situation often. If you had a very difficult day at work, you are tired, and your child misbehaves, you probably will have less patience than if the incident happened on Saturday morning. You are human, and there are limits to your patience, based on your state of mind and the previous behavior and expectations of your child. The teacher should receive the same consideration, especially if you are volunteering in the classroom and observing normal everyday situations. When you are a volunteer, there must be a matter of trust between you and the teacher, or the volunteering efforts are sure to be curtailed.

5

School Decision Making
and Advocacy

Ms. Dugas was frustrated. The school decision-making council, which was now controlled by a majority of parents, voted to require that all teachers have their students in the school computer lab thirty minutes each week, no matter what. The teachers on the council tried to explain that in elementary school, by the time they got the students in, the computers set up, and instructions given, it was virtually time to leave. As an educationally sound alternative, the teachers wanted each class to have a two-hour block of computer lab time once a month. They explained that this would encompass the same amount of time, but would be much more manageable and worthwhile curricular-wise. Unfortunately, a couple of the parents refused to listen to the teachers' advice and insisted that their children have as much computer time per week as their friends' children have in private school. Ms. Dugas was discouraged. She believed that parents should have a voice in the school, but the teachers' professional opinion should count for something, too.

Ms. Warren was frustrated. Her son was not getting the amount of computer lab time that she felt he needed. She even got herself elected to the school decision-making council to ensure that the teachers did what she felt they should do. Unfortunately, her son's current teacher seemed to find excuses every other week as to why the students couldn't go into the computer lab during their time slot. The teacher's excuses did not fly with her. Ms. Warren felt that if the teacher did a better job, she could manage her classroom. Her son's school was supposed to be one of the best public schools in the district, and if the local private schools could have thirty minutes of computer time a week, she was going to make sure that her son's school would also. After all, she figured, she was the parent, and the teaching staff needed to do what the parents decide.

The Issue

As the result of numerous educational reforms over the last twenty years, along with the recent No Child Left Behind Act (NCLB), parents now have more say in school decision making than ever before. This is not a bad thing. To the contrary, if there is to be a true partnership between the school and the home, then parents should have a voice in school matters. The problem arises when roles for teachers, administrators, and parents are not clearly defined and delineated—and respected. That is the critical element. Decision making can be shared successfully among these parties only when an element of trust and respect is present.

One of the questions asked on the questionnaire used for researching this book was "How can parents best be involved in school decision making and advocacy?"

The two most common responses from both teachers and parents were some form of:

- Attend school meetings
- Join/participate in the PTA

(Mandel 2006b)

Neither one of these ideas truly involves parents in the school decision-making process. One, attend school meetings, is basically informational. The other, join/participate in the PTA, is mainly service-based.

Both the parents and the school staff fulfill critical roles in the school decision-making process. Parents are the primary stakeholders. It is *their* children who are being influenced by the school's educational program and personnel. They have an interest at the most basic level in what occurs within the school. Many of them are also highly educated professionals. However, herein lies the twofold problem:

1. Parents want what is best for their child, regardless of whether or not it may be what is best for the overall school program, or whether it impacts others.
2. While parents may be highly educated professionals in their fields, they do not possess the same body of knowledge in the field of education.

Teachers are also highly educated professionals. The vast majority of them have completed course work well beyond a bachelor's degree. All have specialized credentialing in their fields. In fact, one of the most controversial elements of NCLB is the placement of a "highly qualified" teacher in every classroom.

In order for a partnership between teachers and parents to work, each side must trust and respect the other. Otherwise, a good portion of everyone's time will be spent trying to determine the hidden agenda of the other side.

Here is an analogy regarding the two types of schools that can be created based on this philosophy. I call it the Tale of Two Schools—a true story of two public schools.

School A and School B were in identical socioeconomic areas, suburban upper-middle class. Both had very active parents, and both had a good deal of extra money at their disposal due to the parents' efforts. However, School A had higher test scores and a significantly better reputation. Why? The answer lies in a basic philosophical difference between the two.

In School A, the principal and teachers ran the school. The parents were there for support. Sure, they were on the school decision-making councils and had input into decisions, but they realized that their primary role was to provide advice and support to the educators. They offered their opinions—which were always considered, but not always followed—and they followed through with assisting with anything the school personnel requested. As a direct result, at this school, test scores were high, staff and students were happy, and the school was viewed as one of the best in the district.

School B was three miles and light-years away. In this school, the parents ran the school, and the staff was there to support. The parents made most of the decisions on the school decision-making councils, and if they did not get their way on something, a simple phone call to the principal's superiors usually changed all decisions to their liking. A few parents ran a drama program and had the freedom to remove any child from any classroom at any time for rehearsal. One principal attempted to gain control over this program by hiring a teacher with drama background to supervise the program. When the parents found out, they called an immediate meeting with the principal, demanded that the teacher not be hired, and the transfer was ultimately canceled (even though it had already been district approved). At this school, test scores were relatively high (but not as high as School A), the principal left every few years due to frustration, and teacher turnover was more than the district average. Although the school was in a very nice neighborhood, it had a lousy reputation.

This is a true story of the different ways that parents can be involved in the decision-making processes of the school. In a true partnership, all parties have distinct and divergent roles that must be respected. An analogy to the business world illustrates this point:

Position	Role	Function
Owner	To set overall policy for the company	To ensure that the company is on course to produce a product desired by the consumers
Managers	To make the company run efficiently and successfully	Based on their skills and knowledge in the field, to successfully implement company policy
Workers	To work, based on the company's program	To work to their best ability to make the company as successful as possible
Consumers	To buy into the importance of the product	To let the owner know what characteristics they desire and do not desire so that they buy the product

There are four definitive roles in any large, successful business. Each one has an important part in the business's ultimate success.

Each of these four roles is distinct and critical to the running of a successful business. And more important, each one is integrated into the other. For example:

- The owner must set company policy based on what consumers want and then hire competent managers and allow them to use their skills and knowledge to implement the policies.

- The managers must implement company policy while making the workers happy so as to be productive.
- The workers must be happy in order to produce at their capabilities, thereby creating the best product possible.
- The consumers must let the owner know what they want and do not want, through the purchase (or non-purchase) of the product.

In many ways, the roles of the various elements of the school operate in the same fashion. The product, however, is not a tangible item but instead higher test scores and greater student achievement. Using the identical analogy:

Position	Role	Function
Administrator (Owner)	To set overall policy for the school	To ensure that the school is on course to produce the type of student achievement desired by the parents
Teachers (Managers)	To make the school run efficiently and successfully	Based on their skills and knowledge in the field, to successfully implement school policy
Students (Workers)	To learn, based on the school program	To learn to their best ability to make the school as successful as possible

| Parents (Consumers) | To buy into the importance of the educational program | To let the administrator know what aspects they desire and do not desire so that they support the school program |

As with the business analogy, each of these four roles is distinct and critical to the running of a successful educational program. And more important, each one is integrated into the other. For example:

- The administrator must set school policy based on what parents want and then hire competent teachers and allow them to use their skills and knowledge to implement the policies.
- The teachers must implement school policy while making the students happy so as to be productive.
- The students must be happy in order to produce at their capabilities, thereby achieving at the best level possible.
- The parents must let the administrator know what they want and do not want, through their support (or non-support) of the school program.

The balance of this chapter suggests ways that this partnership can be fostered so that parents can fully participate in school decision making and advocacy. It focuses on specific responsibilities that both teachers and parents have toward building on each others' strengths in order to improve the school's educational program.

Responsibilities of Teachers and Parents in Decision Making and Advocacy

Both school personnel and parents need to view themselves as collaborative partners in the school's educational program. They need to examine the various aspects of the curricular process and work within their specific areas, without imposing their will on the other.

Good curriculum development is a lengthy process that first looks at the end product—the type of student graduate desired—and then devises the means to obtain that result. There are four distinct components of curriculum development. Each one is a natural continuation of the previous one:

- **Philosophy.** What is the basic philosophy of the school? In what do the parents/community believe? *Determination of the philosophy of the school is a parent responsibility based on the mores and culture of the community.*
- **Goals.** What is the type of student that will graduate from the school? What are the important attributes that a graduate of the school should have? *Determination of the goals of the school is a parent responsibility based on the mores and culture of the community.*
- **Objectives.** How do the goals get implemented? What concrete guidelines are needed to activate these goals? *Determination of the objectives is an administrator/teacher responsibility based on the professional knowledge gleaned from years of education and experience.*
- **Methods.** How are the objectives implemented within the classroom? How is the educational program taught? *Determination of the methods is a teacher responsibility based on the professional knowledge gleaned from years of education and experience.*

Parents (the community) are primarily responsible for the overall philosophy and goals of the educational program. The school personnel are primarily responsible for the implementation of that program through establishment of objectives and teaching methodologies. It is when one side does not respect this demarcation of roles and imposes its will on the other that problems arise.

As illustrated in the above examples, you can see that there is a tremendous variation as to the delineation of these roles. The quality and quantity of parent involvement varies greatly from school to school. The amount of support and encouragement that parent involvement is given by school personnel also varies greatly from school to school.

One final illustration of a successful school decision-making program comes from a highly rated suburban private school. This institution has a school board that makes most overall, broad educational decisions (the philosophies and goals listed above). However, there are two important requirements for becoming a member of this school board: the person must be in the field of education in some fashion, and the person may not have a child currently in the school.

While this is obviously an extreme case, the concepts behind these requirements are important to note and implement on all school decision-making bodies:

1. Decision making must be *informed* decision making.
2. There can be no conflict of interest between the decision makers' personal agendas and their educational/school decisions.

Informed decision making and removing conflict of interest are critical components for any successful school decision-making and advocacy program. Both teachers and parents have a duty to make this partnership as successful as possible.

For the Teacher

- **Educating parents.** For parents to be involved in decision making and advocacy, they must be educated in those areas. While this is normally a responsibility of the administration—if it is done at all—your parents have their greatest school contact through you.

There are a number of different levels of education you can provide for your students' parents. A basic one is a parent orientation, similar to new student orientation in the sixth or ninth grades. Besides the normal curricular and school policy issues, you can also discuss avenues that parents may pursue when they experience a problem. You can share information about school services and people or agencies to contact if parents have problems in areas as diverse as personal difficulties (financial, medical, legal), school policy decisions (councils, administrators), or your classroom (how to go through the proper channels). The school, and the overall educational community, can be a rather complex organization. Parents often need to be taught how to most productively raise issues, the best procedures to follow, and what follow-up measures are at their disposal.

■ **Get personally involved in the overall educational community.** Become informed and involved in national, state, and local educational issues. There are many issues for which your voice is important. Too often, teachers leave out-of-the-classroom issues for "someone else." In today's society, more than any other previous one, our strength is in numbers. Public education, and teachers in particular, are being attacked from all sides. We need to stand up for our rights, to stand up for what we know is best for our students, our classrooms, and our schools. We cannot expect parents to be our public advocates if we do not lead by example. This means that teachers have a responsibility to stay informed about current events in educational topics, and participate, when needed, in shaping educational policies.

One of the easiest and most efficient ways to keep up-to-date on daily events in the field of education is by subscribing to an electronic newsletter entitled *ASCD SmartBrief,* published by the Association for Supervision and Curriculum Development (ASCD). Sent by e-mail, this newsletter contains brief summaries of issues from newspapers and periodicals throughout the nation, along with links to the original article if you want to go into greater detail. An example of one of its summaries follows.

Some Experts View Technology as a Mixed Blessing

Technology has enhanced young people's ability to multitask and research, but it has also hurt the quality of student papers by making it too easy to cut and paste in text, some experts say. Other observers, however, argue that technology has made learning more exciting. *Chicago Tribune*

—*ASCD SmartBrief* (2006)

By clicking on the words *Chicago Tribune*, you are immediately linked to the entire article. With a subscription to this free newsletter, you can be kept up-to-date on current educational happenings throughout the country . You can sign up for this newsletter on the ASCD Web site at www.ascd.org. Click on the News and Issues link, and then Subscribe Today.

■ **Get involved at the school site.** Teachers often go through a cycle of involvement at their school site. For the first few years, new teachers usually do not get involved with school decision-making committees, as they have too much to do in their classroom or feel that they do not yet know enough to fully participate. Then they begin to join the committees and become full members for a number of years, until they become frustrated with administrative personnel or the committee's lack of real power. When they ultimately feel that their participation is a waste of time, they drop out. For the rest of their stay at the school, wild horses cannot drag them back onto the committees. (One exception is program coordinators, who have their own agenda for serving on the committees, or those considered administrative "yes" people, who are recruited by some administrators to ensure that votes on the committees go a certain way.)

This is obviously a simplistic, generalized description of teacher participation. However, I am sure that you have seen many of these people at your school site.

The fact is, in today's educational environment, where community-based decision-making committees have a greater say in school matters than ever before, it is the experienced teacher who needs to volunteer and participate. Teachers need to have their voices heard, and promote teacher-based positions, protecting an integral part of the argument on any issue. Consensus is critical for decision-making committees to work productively and positively for the school program. And this consensus must come from sharing, listening to, and resolving differences among all three partners—teachers, administrators, and parents. If the school's best teachers are not on the committees, how will your opinions and positions be presented? When your most experienced teachers are not on the committee, decisions made that are not popular with the teaching staff are nobody's fault but the overall teaching staff's.

Another avenue for teachers to get involved in is membership in the local teachers' union. You may not agree with many of the union's positions. However, they are your representatives, and they do look after your overall interests in the long run. The teachers' union is very similar to the American system of representative democracy. We elect representatives who theoretically pursue our interests in legislative bodies. We may not agree with all of their decisions or votes, but overall, they represent us. If they do not represent their constituents the majority of the time, we can vote them out of office. Support of the union is very similar. The union is your number one advocate, especially in district- and state-level matters, such as funding for salaries and benefits, and improving working conditions. You have to ask yourself, who else is going to support your overall interests?

For the Parent

■ **Get involved at school for the school.** Parent participation in school decision making works only when the parent participates for the betterment of the child's school, versus for the betterment of the individual child. That is a very important distinction. When parents get involved as the agent of their child, conflicts quickly arise and respect is lost among all parties. This

Parent Tip

How to Make Your Voice Sway Public Opinion

Too often the media, especially the print media, are very negative toward schools. Your voice, through letters to the editor and opinion pieces, can help sway public opinion toward more pro-education stances, or can shed light on one-sided reporting.

You can locate newspaper, radio, and television addresses in your area by going to the Yahoo! Web site, and following these links:

- Go to Yahoo (www.yahoo.com).
- Select the Directory link on top under the More button.
- Go down to the News & Media link.
- Click on By Region, then U.S. States, then select your personal state.
- Select either Newspapers, Radio, or Television.

Search for those outlets in your local area, and write your pro-education piece. It's that easy!

school-first mind-set is a crucial first step that must be accomplished if there is to be a productive and positive partnership between parents and the school personnel in decision-making activities.

However, if an issue arises where you do not feel you can be an objective participant because it directly involves your child, simply excuse yourself from the discussion. You will earn tremendous respect from the school staff, and your opinion will be considered even more valuable during other discussions and topics.

If you find it impossible to get involved in decision-making committees due to your work schedule, talk to the administrator about the possibility of having some committee meetings held in the evening so the voices of working parents can be heard. You may not be able to become a full member of the committee, but you can still contribute as a guest at meetings. Occasional evening meetings are a wonderful way to offer an opportunity for all parents to participate in school decision making and functions.

Getting parents actively involved can begin through a type of "PTA at Night" program. Many PTA duties that are conducted during the day by parents who do not work outside of the house can also be scheduled for the evening. Evening work on a fund-raiser or a mailing can be scheduled for seven to nine in the evening rather than nine to eleven in the morning so that other parents can become involved. It may also significantly boost the number of PTA volunteers at a school, since their numbers are usually limited to those parents who do not work or who have very flexible hours during the day. Once you have a greater representation at PTA events, many of these newly involved parents can move to involvement in decision making and advocacy.

■ **Get personally involved in the overall educational community.** As is true for teachers, you as a parent can and should be a tremendous advocate of educational issues that affect your child's school. There are two critical components of this involvement: information and action.

The first step toward becoming involved in educational issues is to make yourself aware of these issues. You can request that the school's administration regularly supply parents with contemporary educational articles of interest. There are also a couple of ways that you can educate yourself on topics of interest. See the For the Teacher section on page 88 for information on a free daily electronic educational newsletter called the *ASCD SmartBrief* that can easily keep you abreast of educational current events.

An excellent educational journal titled *Educational Leadership* is published by the Association for Supervision and Curriculum Development

(ASCD). While you have to join the ASCD to receive this periodical, it is a worthwhile investment for keeping up-to-date with major issues in education. The periodical is easy to read (limited in educational jargon) and always current with contributions from some of the top authors and educators in the country. For example, some of the recent topics of special interest to parents have included: "Challenging the Status Quo," "NCLB: Taking Stock, Looking Forward," "Responding to Changing Demographics," and "The Prepared Graduate." Information about this periodical is available on the ASCD Web site (www.ascd.org). Click on Publications and then Educational Leadership.

Once you have become acquainted with the issues, it is important that you use your newfound knowledge. Taking action and becoming an advocate for your child's school is one of the best ways you can channel your energies toward the betterment of the educational program.

Write, e-mail, or call your congressperson or state representative on a regular basis about educational issues. Elected officials listen to their constituents, especially about community issues. How they vote generally depends on how many letters, e-mails, or calls they receive from people in their district. By taking as little as fifteen to twenty minutes at a time, you can have a direct influence on these votes by being vocal and active.

Learn how to contact your representative and how they vote on educational issues by going to the Web site Project Vote-Smart (http://vote-smart.org). By simply typing in your representative's name or your zip code, you will get links to information about them, including how to contact them. This service includes not only the representatives in Congress but also those in every state legislature in the country.

The easiest, and probably most efficient, way to investigate your representative's positions on various issues is by noticing how your representative is rated by various interest groups. Click on the link to Interest Group Ratings. These lobbyists rate the person on how often they voted on issues with which they were concerned. The higher the percentage, the more that person votes in favor of their particular issues. Scroll down to Education. You will see ratings by the following organizations:

- National Education Association
- National Parent Teacher Association
- National School Boards Association

The higher the percentage these organizations give to your representative, the more they vote in favor of educational issues. (Be aware that there are some discrepancies with each group. The NEA is solely teacher based, the PTA is mostly parent based with teacher input, and the NSBA is administrator based.)

Based on this information, you can contact your representative to either encourage a more proactive stance on educational issues or work to put a more education-friendly person in that office. In this fashion, you, as a parent and a voter, can become one of the best advocates for your child's school.

6

Collaborating with Community

Ms. Cook was frustrated. She taught at an economically disadvantaged school that was continuously short on supplies and money. In addition, her students had no role models within the community—no sense of belonging to the greater whole. As she drove home each day, she passed many local businesses. She noticed that the majority of them seemed to be successful and popular. She started to wonder how she could get these businesspeople involved with supporting their neighborhood school, both financially and by serving as some form of mentors for her students.

Ms. Silva was frustrated. Her son was not focused. Sure, he passed his classes, but he had no desire to work toward his future. He did not want to go to college and did not demonstrate any desire to go into any type of profession. The Silvas lived in an immigrant community. There were many first-generation businesses owned by successful neighborhood people who could serve as role models for her son. She could not understand why the school did not get these people involved in the school program so that students like her son could have some positive direction from their neighborhood.

The Issue

The immediate neighborhood community around the school is an extremely valuable resource for the educational program. Whether your school is located in a wealthy or a poor neighborhood, whether it has long-established residents or houses first-generation Americans, community members can become partners, enhancing the school program through their services, their expertise, and their finances.

Again, as is true for much of the material in this book, the root of the issue is the attitude one group holds toward the other. How does the school look at the community? How does the community view the school? One of two possible attitudes will be derived from this evaluation:

■ The school is *located in* the community.
■ The school is a *part of* the community.

The attitudes are significantly different. In the first, there is little connection between the school and the community other than an address. The children who live within these preset school boundaries attend that particular school. There is little if any interaction with the local community, other than what community members generate through their children's school activities. In this scenario, members of the community without children only come into contact with the school when it serves as a polling place for an election. They feel little connection to the school, and it shows when local bond issues come up for a vote. Many local residents might consider the school a nuisance. Obviously, this type of school is not involved in any sort of partnership with the community—there is no collaboration of any form between the two.

The second example is diametrically opposite of the first. In this scenario, the school views itself as an intricate part of the community, and the community considers it "its" school. The school treats the community as a resource, and the community looks at the school with pride, something that makes the entire community better. Members of both know and respect each other, and turn to the other for assistance when necessary. A true partnership exists.

Growing up in suburban Cleveland, Ohio, my father always maintained that the worth of a neighborhood was seen through its schools. Until the 1980s, bond issues never failed. Real estate agents used the local school as the most important selling point of a house, whether or not the prospective buyer had children. This is the type of partnership that schools need to strive for with their local community: a true collaboration. And it starts with getting to know each other.

This chapter is not divided into teacher and parent sections. The "school" refers to the teachers, along with all of the programs in which they are involved. The "community" includes the parents, but it goes beyond parents to those who do not have children at the school.

Getting to Know the Community

It is impossible to get the community involved in the school program if the teaching staff knows little about the community. In most larger cities, the majority of the staff does not live within walking distance of the school. This is true even more often for schools located in lower socioeconomic neighborhoods.

For example, a typical middle school in a suburban, lower socioeconomic neighborhood in Los Angeles has 109 credentialed staff members. Of those 109, only 6 (5.5 percent) live within the same zip code of the school, much less within walking distance.

In order to understand the students better, in order to appreciate the resources of the community, teachers need to make it a point to get to know the community. Here are some ways to do so.

- **Take a walking tour.** The easiest way to get to know the community is to take a simple walking tour. Even if the neighborhood is not the best, a group of teachers walking through together would be safe in the majority of communities.

  The best time to take this type of tour is during the teacher orientation days before the start of the formal school year. Small groups of teachers can walk down the major streets around the school and stop in the various stores and businesses. They can meet community members and introduce themselves. Then they can start a discussion on how the community can become involved in the school, and discover how the school can become involved with members of the community. This first contact establishes positive attitudes among all parties. The community members get to know that these "outsiders" who teach at the local school are real people and truly interested in them. More important, the teachers get to discover more about the backgrounds of their students, and the resources that are available in the school's surroundings.

- **Learn the different cultures of the community.** Teachers should ask themselves, "Who is the community?" They need to learn about the various cultures residing in the area. One of the best ways to do so is to visit the area on a Sunday. Go to one of the community parks or drive through some of the neighborhoods. Observe the family life that goes on. Community members will certainly feel that you care about the students' lives, and you will gain more knowledge about what is important in the students' lives. Remember, the more you know about your students—including their outside lives—the more you can help them better achieve.

  If you know that your community has a substantial ethnic population, make it a point to visit during one of their holidays or celebrations. The newspaper or local community centers are sure to have the particulars for these events. Some simple examples are visiting a Cinco de Mayo festival in a Mexican neighborhood, a New Year's parade in a Chinese neighborhood, a commemorative celebration on Martin Luther King Jr. Day in an African American neighborhood, and a Purim carnival in a Jewish neighborhood. All of these experiences will teach you about the rich cultures of your school's community, and at the same time your attendance will help forge a partnership with the members of that community and the school.

■ **Create a family Community Resource Guide.** Very often families in your school are not familiar with many of the resources in their community. Creating and distributing a Community Resource Guide can be extremely helpful for these families.

This guide should contain many harder-to-locate places of interest, rather than the obvious (such as supermarkets or shopping malls). Things of this nature would include local places to pay utilities, free medical clinics, various social services, and family recreational opportunities such as small parks or community centers. You can also include locations that directly tie to the students' educational program, such as local libraries and museums.

You can locate many of these services easily during your visits, or by using other community resource lists. Or, try a community search through the Yahoo! Internet site (www.yahoo.com). This online resource will provide you with community-based categories you can explore to locate additional neighborhood resources.

Getting the Community to Know the School

Just as the school should have pride in its community, the community should have pride in the school. When the local population has pride in their school—notice I said "their" school rather than "the" school—they are more apt to support the

Teacher Tip
How to Publicize Test Scores to the Community

Probably the single most important item involved in the entire issue of raising test scores concerns how the scores are actually reported and, more important, interpreted. Schools frequently improve their scores but come off poorly (seemingly displaying no improvement) because of the way the scores are usually reported and discussed through the use of percentiles.

■ **The problems with percentiles.** Using percentiles to report, analyze, and discuss school progress is a significant problem for many institutions. They are inherently unfair to those in low socioeconomic areas where achievement has been problematic due to either large non-English-speaking immigrant populations or inner-city neighborhoods suffering from poor economic conditions.

Percentiles rank schools in comparison with other schools that take the same statewide exam. The schools that score in the lower 10 percent on the state exam will fall into the first percentile. The schools ranking in the 11 to 20 percent range fall into the second percentile, and so on, up to ten. Unfortunately, school demographics or location are not taken into account, only test scores.

The problem with this ranking system is that if a school improves, that improvement may not be evident if other schools also improve. With percentiles, no matter how much each school succeeds in raising its scores and improving student achievement, one will always be ranked at the bottom!

■ **Using raw scores to show actual improvement.** The precise numeric raw score is how school improvement is actually displayed. A school that has gone from a 320 to a 385 has improved not only sixty-five points, but has demonstrated a 20 percent increase in its scores! That is a huge improvement, even if the school is still considered to be in the lowest percentile overall for their district.

As long as the raw scores are based on the same scale from year to year (for example, the entire test may be worth eight hundred points every year), you can legitimately use the data to compare one year to the next.

(Mandel 2006a)

educational program with both their time and their money. In addition, pride in the local school increases property values, bringing even more money and resources into the neighborhood, and ultimately to the school.

■ **Publicize school events and achievements.** It is primarily incumbent upon the school to create positive public relations for itself within the community. The school should regulary send press releases and positive reports to the local newspapers. Flyers and posters for shows and special events should be displayed prominently throughout the neighborhood. The school should also personally invite local businesspeople to these events.

Ultimately, the school can become a form of local cultural arts center, where neighborhood residents regularly attend concerts, shows, and special programs.

■ **Create a school brochure.** A brochure highlighting the best aspects of the school can be created to publicize the following types of items:

- Special programs offered by the school
- Increases in local test scores
- School events that are open to the community
- A description of the student body and the special qualifications of the faculty

With simple computer programs such as Adobe Photoshop and InDesign, along with a digital camera, you can create a colorful, fairly inexpensive brochure that includes photos of the school and its programs. This brochure can be distributed throughout the community and available in local business establishments.

This type of publicity has a number of important benefits. The most obvious are to let the community know about the school and develop pride in its accomplishments. Another benefit is to make your school desirable to parents. One aspect of the No Child Left Behind Act (NCLB) is allowing parents the opportunity to transfer their children to a higher performing, more desirable school. If your school is well known as a good institution, you can increase your enrollment through these transfers. Obviously, if your school is at capacity, this becomes irrelevant. However, if you have openings, more students enrolled translates into an increase in state money, which then allows you to add or expand educational programs within the school.

Establishing a True Partnership with the Community

Once the school staff knows and supports the community, and the community knows and supports the school, a true partnership can be established. Just as with a partnership between teachers and parents, this school and community partnership goes well beyond just informing and inviting.

Be aware that when larger corporations become involved with the school, certain ground rules must be established so that neither students nor the school are used inappropriately. The National PTA established the following guidelines in its corporate sponsorship policy and resolution, "Commercial Exploitation of Students in Schools":

- Corporate involvement must support the goals and objectives of the school. Curriculum and instruction are within the purview of educators.
- Corporate involvement programs must be structured to meet an identified need; linked to specific activities, events, and programs—not a commercial motive; and evaluated for effectiveness by the school or district on an ongoing basis.
- Because school property and time are publicly funded, corporate involvement should not sell or provide free access to advertisements on school property or require students to observe, listen to, or read commercial advertising as a condition of the school receiving a donation of money or equipment.

- Educators should hold sponsored and donated materials to the same standards used for the selection and purchase of other school-related materials. The materials should offer balanced and diverse views.
- Corporate involvement programs should not limit the discretion of educators in the use of sponsored materials.
- Sponsor recognition and corporate logos should be used for identification rather than commercial purposes.

(National PTA 2000)

The ultimate goal in collaborating with the community is to establish a relationship where the community is actively involved in improving the educational program of the school, and the school is actively involved in improving the local community. Many of the following ideas can be implemented by individual teachers or parents. A number of them are school-based and must be presented—and promoted—to administrators or brought up to school-based councils. Do not make the mistake of feeling that since some of these ideas are beyond one's scope that they are irrelevant to you. A positive partnership with the community benefits everybody involved, and you as a teacher or parent can promote these ideas to effect positive change.

- **Get the community into the school.** There are a number of important steps to take in establishing this new partnership. The most popular way of involving community members is to integrate them into the school population. This can be accomplished a number of ways, ranging from having them share their expertise with the students to having them actively participate in the established school program.

  One way to display the expertise of community members is to hold an annual Community Day. On this day, members of the community come to the school and talk to students about what they do in their profession, as well as share information about resources that they provide to the community.

Depending on the number of volunteers you have and the age of the students, the speakers can travel from one classroom to another on a set schedule, or join together in a form of an assembly.

Instead of a special Community Day, teachers can place community speakers into the school curriculum. The most obvious use of neighborhood community member visitations is during primary grade topics such as the community (police, firefighters, shopkeepers). However, individuals from the community can also be incorporated into more advanced sections of the curriculum. For example:

- A blind community member with a guide dog can enhance a literature piece dealing with the blind, such as the book *Follow My Leader* (Garfield 1957).
- A local botanist can talk about photosynthesis, genetics, or biochemistry in a science class.
- A Muslim or Catholic cleric can discuss the Crusades or religious life in the Middle Ages.
- A chef can visit a math class and discuss how multiplying fractions is a real-world necessity when dealing with large recipes.

A little creativity and planning can bring these community curricular resources directly into the classroom as an excellent real-life enhancement to the educational program.

Local senior citizens are another resource that can assist in the classroom. A significant number of these people were professionals when they were working—and many of them were teachers. These potential volunteers often can be incorporated as classroom aides or tutors, using their time and resources to help your students directly. (Be sure to incorporate the ideas presented in the chapter on volunteering when using these volunteers.)

Another way to get community members into the school is with special projects or events. For example, they can be judges for science or art fairs, or help run school carnivals or other large schoolwide events.

You can keep community members informed of school programs with a community e-mail list. Most businesses and professionals have e-mail addresses. By accumulating a list of these addresses, you can create a mass mailing list that you can use to regularly send information about the school and its events. This is an easy way to publicize the great things happening at your school. Plus, you can also use this list to send out a call for help when you need resources or people.

Whether you are using their expertise directly in the curriculum or their time for classroom or school assistance, you should actively work on getting community members involved in the school program.

■ **Get the school into the community.** Just as you want to get community members involved in the school program, if you want a true partnership to exist it is just as important to get the school involved in the community. Students, especially those on the secondary level, need to learn about the concept of community service, and that they as neighborhood residents have a place in the greater community. Subsequently, the community will see the school as an important, valuable, and intricate part of their neighborhood. This in turn could lead to greater support for the educational program—both in community volunteering and in the voting booth when school bond issues are on the ballot.

Once you know your community well and are familiar with the professionals and organizations working in your area, explore the possibility of establishing internships for your students. This is especially applicable to high school students who are beginning to think about their future careers. Many local professionals, businesses, and organizations will be willing to have your students volunteer to learn about the services they provide.

Many of these volunteer opportunities can eventually turn into paying jobs for your students. More important, these internships can give your students direction into later careers, motivating them to take advantage of higher educational opportunities—be it college or advanced trade school education in a specific area.

While internships are most valuable for high school students, all school levels can get involved in community service projects. Unfortunately, many teachers do not know about all of the opportunities available in the local area, and therefore concentrate on only the most obvious, such as a local food bank. As a result, many excellent service possibilities go unexplored. Luckily, there is an excellent Web site called Volunteer Match that lists virtually all of the community service opportunities in a neighborhood.

Volunteer Match (www.volunteermatch.org) is very simple to use. Type in your school's zip code and how far you are willing to travel for the volunteer work (five, ten, twenty miles, or city, county, metro area). Then select the types of volunteer work you want to explore. Categories include children and youth, crisis support, disabled, environment, homeless, hunger, hurricane relief, immigrants, seniors, and many more. As of this writing, the service has already made close to three million referrals, and about forty thousand volunteer opportunities are currently listed.

Once you input your information, the site provides you with a list of opportunities. Each one lists the name of the sponsoring organization, the types of volunteers they need, addresses and contact information, hours for the volunteer work, and maps. Everything you could possibly need to get your students involved in a community service opportunity is provided for you.

■ **Using the financial resources of the community.** Sometimes the most important thing that the school needs from the community is money. In this era of limited budgets for education, many supplemental programs—especially in the arts—have been eliminated from the overall educational program. Supplemental resources, field trips, and other "non-core" expenses have also suffered. The financial resources of the community can significantly fill the void left by current limits and restrictions on school funding.

There are many ways in which the school can raise community funds. Unfortunately, much of your fund-raising ability depends on the particular community in which the school is located. You need to make certain determinations about your socioeconomic area and the types of assistance that would be reasonable to expect.

Also, an important differentiation is being made here between fund-raising that is community based versus parent based. Gift drives and candy sales are the types of fund-raising that are parent based—parents, their work places, relatives, or direct neighbors are those that generally fund these activities. Community-based fundraising involves the finances outside of the immediate school community.

Some fairly common community fund-raising activities include the following:

- *An ad book*. Schools can put together an ad book if there are numerous businesses in the community. Businesses or professionals purchase an eighth of a page (business card size), a fourth, a half, or a full page. They design an ad for their business (preferably in electronic form). Using a simple computer layout design program such as Adobe InDesign, the ads are put together in a pamphlet and distributed throughout the entire school population. The ad buyers gain welcome publicity for their businesses as the school population shows its appreciation for the support. Soliciting ads for this type of campaign is especially productive in November and December—the end of the tax year—as these donations are generally tax-deductible.
- *Restaurant dinners*. Many local restaurants, both sit-down and fast food, will donate a percentage of their sales over a specific time period to a

local school. For example, you can get a local Mexican restaurant to donate 25 percent of all sales between four and eight o'clock on a specific school fundraising night. The school simply must publicize the event. It is an easy, no-work fundraiser for the school, and the restaurant gets extra business on a normally slow weekday evening.

■ *Street fairs.* If you have a fairly large retail area, local merchants can band together to sponsor a street fair. These large events can be organized by a local council or chamber of commerce. All of the event proceeds can be earmarked to raise money for a number of neighborhood schools.

■ **Partnership programs.** You can start an "I'm a Partner of _____ School" program with local businesses. The businesses become a sponsor of the school through donating a predetermined amount of money. They are then provided with a sticker or sign for display in their window, along with other perks such as free tickets to all school shows, or their name printed on the back of a school shirt. You can conduct a schoolwide campaign to promote those businesses among your school families. The school gains additional funds, and the local businesses gain additional patronage as school families specifically use their services as a result of their support. Again, this type of campaign works well toward the end of the tax year.

Local businesses can also use their resources to purchase supplies at cost for the school. Many businesses get wholesale rates that can be passed on to the local school for supplies for which they would normally have to pay retail. Paper, printer cartridges, calculators, CD-ROMS, and other office supplies are just some of the types of materials that can be purchased for the local school through a partnership with neighborhood businesses.

Teacher Tip
A Community-Based Learning Experience

There are a number of different activities that can get your students involved in the community. Teachers and parents should attempt to get students into the community whenever possible in order to establish a true partnership.

This following activity was submitted on one of the questionnaires acquired in the research of this book:

The first grade teacher at my children's school has her class walk to the local supermarket every year and do an apple parade. They prepare for two weeks for this field trip by making apple print T-shirts, making apple rhyme books, and reading stories and learning songs that have to do with apples. While at the store, they put on a little program for the store customers by singing the songs that they learned. They get to have an apple tasting session with the produce guy, where they taste every kind of apple that the store carries and they vote on the one that they like the most. Then, afterward, they go back to class and make homemade applesauce and have a party with their classmates. I think that it is great that this teacher has this connection into the community and takes her teaching outside of the four walls along with her students.

—Teacher, Bellevue, Washington (Mandel 2006b)

7

Respect

Ms. Ferry was frustrated. Teaching was something she loved more than anything in the world. It was her calling, her passion. But she was getting perturbed about the lack of respect that she received from parents. She taught at a good, upper-middle class suburban school with students who traditionally enjoyed high test scores. However, she was ready to transfer over to an inner-city school simply to get away from the parents. It seemed as if anytime she gave a grade less than a *B*, she was questioned. The day before, a mother confronted her, upset that her daughter's *A* on a test was not high enough! A number of the parents continually hovered around her classroom, and if they saw something they did not like, they immediately ran to the principal. Worse than that was the disrespect they exhibited toward her in person. Once, she actually overheard a couple of the parents talking about her. They said if she's that smart, why is she teaching? Ms. Ferry was frustrated. Her teacher friends who were jealous that she was at such a "good" school had no concept of what life was really like at that institution.

Ms. Fox was frustrated. She was a single parent, working full-time, trying to raise two daughters and deal with an ex-husband who was continually fighting her about his financial support. She rarely returned home before six o'clock. Exhausted, she had to make dinner, take care of household chores, and ultimately battle with her children about their homework. She planned on attending Back-to-School Night, but it had been a horrible day at work, she had a major fight with her ex-husband on the phone on the way home, and was exhausted, depressed, and utterly aggravated. She simply did not make it to school that evening. The next day her youngest daughter came home crying because her teacher said that the parents who didn't show up the previous night obviously did not care about their child's education. Ms. Fox was frustrated. This teacher who was so obviously judgmental had no concept of the reality for some parents who were struggling with day-to-day life.

The Issue

A major thread running throughout all of the chapters in this book has been that mutual respect between teachers and parents is critical in order for a true partnership to exist. While many will say that respect is earned, the fact is it is also automatically deserved. I believe that respect is a granted, and that only disrespect is earned. It is a subtle but significant difference. Teachers and parents must enter their relationship with mutual respect. Otherwise, every questionable encounter will automatically be viewed negatively.

When reading through all of the teacher and parent questionnaires contributed for this book, the level of respect—or lack of respect—that certain teachers and parents had toward the other was obvious. The responses ran the gamut, from extremely positive to extremely negative. Two specific questionnaire responses, however, stood out for the incredible disrespect they demonstrated. These deserve a review:

Teacher Responses   *Parent Responses**

1. **Communication:** Describe what you feel Teacher-Parent communication should be like throughout the school year.

   The teacher, parent, and child all need to be on the "same page."

   Communication should flow from the teachers to the parent's status and needs.

2. **Parenting:** What types of parenting help/suggestions can the teacher offer to help parents with their parenting abilities?

   [Use a] 2 × 4

   None, it's the parent's job to be the parent.

3. **Student Learning:** How can teachers help parents participate more in their students' learning?

   Parents need to know that it doesn't matter if they do not know how to do their child's work, only that they need to oversee that their child completes it.

   I would dismiss the premise of the question because parents have no say in the curriculum.

4. **Volunteering:** What are the most helpful/beneficial ways in which parents can assist the teacher through volunteering of time and/or resources?

   Please stay out of my classroom.

   Teachers need to reach out for help from the parents.

5. **School Decision Making and Advocacy:** How can parents best be involved in school decision making and advocacy?

   Please stay away from decision making. Parents just do not know or understand what is involved.

   How are the decisions made currently? Where are the parents in this process?

6. **Collaborating with the Community:** How can teachers best collaborate with the school community?

   Individual teachers need to observe their students in a non-school setting such as sports or drama/theater arts, etc.

   The question is how do we make teachers more accountable to parents.

7. **Respect:** Please answer as a teacher or parent—What advice/knowledge/insights can you share that will better help teachers respect the parent, or better help the parent respect the teacher?

   Parents are responsible for parenting and their child's behavior and academic effort.

   Parents—make teachers accountable. Teachers—don't bite the hand that feeds you.

*Please also note, the first line of the questionnaire directions was "The purpose of this voluntary questionnaire is to gather. . . ." This parent circled the word voluntary in red and placed a question mark above it.

(Mandel 2006b)

Unfortunately, too many teachers and parents have these types of attitudes toward each other. These attitudes foster a climate of distrust. As a result, a true partnership will never be established between these parties. The child will either become a battleground between the teacher and parent, or will manipulate this mutual distrust to his advantage as he plays one against the other.

Mutual respect leads to trust and cooperation. This does not mean that both parties have to agree all of the time. Parents and teachers need to send the message, "I disagree with you at times, but I support you, because I know you have the child's best interests at heart." That is mutual respect.

The following are issues both teachers and parents should consider. Remember that all relationships are two-sided, and what one party considers respectful or disrespectful may not be what the other considers acceptable or unacceptable. Each party must analyze how its actions are perceived by the other, and work from there to develop the relationship.

I always end my first meeting with new parents at Back-to-School Night with the following statement: "I'll make you a deal. I won't automatically believe what your child says about you, if you don't automatically believe what your child says about me." This puts our relationship for the entire school year into perspective.

Put Yourself in Their Shoes

Contrary to public opinion, both teachers and parents are human. Both have to deal with everyday life. They both have bills to pay, relationships to deal with, and frustrations at work and at home. Respect begins with understanding where the other party is coming from—all of the motivations, agendas, pressures, emotions, problems, and joys that make the person human. Once this is understood and accepted, respect and trust will naturally begin to flow into and throughout the relationship.

For the Teacher

■ **The parents' motivation.** The majority of parents have one basic motivation—their child is the most important thing in the world for them, and they will protect her at all costs, against all threats. If the parent views you as a threat, you will have problems throughout the entire year.

You must get parents to view you as a partner and as an advocate for their child's well-being. Just as they trust the child's pediatrician to take care of her medical needs, they need to trust the child's teacher to take care of her educational needs.

Parents have to feel that you have their child's best interests at heart. This does not mean you always have to be positive in your dealings with the child. Just as a good parent knows when to discipline a child, a teacher must also be negative at times. However, if the parents understand that you are doing something for their child's own good—just as they sometimes must punish their child—then they will be more supportive of your decisions. This is substantially different than happy with all your decisions, which is impossible to have most of the time, especially when their child is receiving negative consequences.

■ **Understand the parents' lives.** In general, the reason a parent is not involved in his child's education is not because he doesn't care. An uninvolved parent is normally uninvolved for a number of reasons. Some of the most prominent reasons include the following:

- *Demands of work.* Whether the parent is a ten-hour-a-day manual laborer or ten-hour-a-day lawyer, physical and mental exhaustion is often a legitimate reason to not be involved in all aspects of the child's education.
- *Single parent/custodial grandparent.* Many single parents are completely overwhelmed with daily life. Many have gone or are going through nasty divorces, which take a tremendous psychological toll on their

lives. Sometimes grandparents are the ones raising the children because of a parent's drug or legal problems. "Becoming involved" in the school often may take second place when the custodial adult is struggling to provide basic daily needs for the child.

- *Lack of English.* Often immigrant parents who do not know English do not become involved because they are embarrassed. These parents are generally supportive of the teacher. However, they limit their involvement at school or at home because they are often embarrassed that their children know English better than they do, or fear that they will embarrass their child by their lack of fluency.

    In order to be more respectful and supportive in the relationship, it is incumbent upon the teacher to understand where the parents are coming from and what they are dealing with in their daily lives.

- **The parents' level of education is irrelevant.** Whether the parents are professionals, whether they have graduate degrees, whether they are immigrant day laborers—their socioeconomic and educational status is irrelevant both to the amount of respect that they deserve, and the amount of respect that you as the teacher may need to demand.

    Often highly educated professionals need to be reminded of your qualifications—that you are not teaching just because you cannot do anything else. They need to realize that you too are a professional. (To this day, I will never forget when a prospective parent came up to me while touring the school and actually asked, "What's a nice Jewish boy with a Ph.D. doing teaching school?")

    "Uneducated" parents often need to be reassured that they are equal to others, that they are concerned and equal partners in their child's education. They need to feel that if there are barriers in language or subject matter knowledge, you will work with them to overcome them in order to establish a partnership with them.

One very simple way to begin to establish an equal relationship is through one's greetings. If the parent refers to you by your title (Mr., Mrs., Miss, Ms.), then you should do the same. On the other hand, if the parent refers to you by your first name, you should address the parent likewise. Something as simple as referring to one's name appropriately can immediately put both parties on the same level, and begin to establish mutual respect.

For the Parent

- **The teacher is an educated professional.** There is little more irritating to a teacher than hearing the old adage, "Those who can do, do; those who can't, teach." It is insulting to the profession, it is insulting to the teacher, and it is simply not true.

  The majority of teachers are professionals. They are there because they love children and they love teaching. Believe me, they are not doing it for the money. And just as with all professions, there are members who really do not belong and who could be considered incompetent. But the majority of teachers are quite competent. They have taken graduate university classes and have earned degrees educating them in how to practice this profession. Unfortunately, situations such as home-schooling cheapen the profession, giving the impression that if anyone can teach, why credential them, and why respect them as professionals?

  Teachers are as intelligent as people in other professions. Unfortunately, American society too often equates one's salary with one's success. This is why teachers are less respected in America than in other countries. Parents need to recognize this and consider the teacher as a professional—one who is helping to improve their family's life, just as their doctor, lawyer, or financial planner helps their family. This is the critical first step toward respect for the teacher.

- **Trust the teacher's professional judgment.** Until a teacher proves otherwise (and occasionally some do), trust should be given from day one—

not the other way around. Teachers genuinely care about their students, even your child.

This concept was beautifully stated on one of the teacher questionnaires submitted for this book:

> Parents need to understand that teachers want all children to succeed. Teachers do not sit around thinking of ways to show vengeance on any student; teachers have entirely too much to do during the day to pick on one child. . . . When discipline problems are constant, then the parent tends to think that the teacher has some personal vendetta against the child and is picking on that child. . . . Teachers do not lie to parents; teachers have nothing to gain from lying to a parent so there is no reason to lie.

> (Mandel 2006b)

■ **Teachers are human.** For all of the reasons stated in the teacher section concerning the lives of parents, teachers, too, are human. They have outside lives, bills to pay, relationships to deal with, and daily life to live. They also have the frustrations inherent in the school and professional realm, from everyday paperwork to the new demands of NCLB.

Ask yourself whether your personal life ever affects your work. Teachers are no different. Understand that their personal lives also can affect their work before you rush to any judgment. Teachers usually do their best, but sometimes they make mistakes. However, if they feel that they have a respectful, nonjudgmental relationship with you, those mistakes can easily be corrected.

Things to Watch For

Most disrespectful behaviors demonstrated by teachers or by parents are not intentional. Usually they involve seemingly innocent actions, which, seen from the other side, are considered disrespectful. Other times they result from inaction—one party not taking the time to understand the other side.

The following are a number of tips that you can use to help establish an environment of respect between the classroom teacher and the parents.

For the Teacher

- **The first week of school.** The first few days of school are an excellent time to get to know the students' families and to have them get to know you. By understanding each other's background, all involved can establish a relationship with a level of respect.

  For students, an early assignment (which also provides an opportunity to demonstrate their writing skills) could be a two-paragraph essay, "About Me." In the first paragraph, the students write about their families. The second paragraph contains information about the students' interests and hobbies. This simple assignment can present you with a tremendous amount of information, especially concerning the makeup of the child's family—divorce, nontraditional, and other variables that may better help you deal with both student and caregivers.

  Also during the first week, you should send home a "portrait" of yourself. Besides the usual goals and classroom policies, this paper should include information about you that would help the parent better understand where you are coming from. Share your professional experiences and accomplishments with the parents. This information will show them that you are a professional. You can also include your expectations of them as parents, establishing guidelines so they clearly know how they can become partners with you in their child's education.

- **Parent conferences.** Students innately will do whatever they can to stay out of trouble, or do their best to limit the amount of trouble they may be in. It is a natural human reaction. Rarely will a parent come home from a parent conference, confront the child, and hear the child say, "The teacher was right. I've been messing up this quarter and it's all my fault." Rather, the child will develop an excuse to limit personal blame. Subsequently, this puts a strain on the relationship between the parent and the teacher, testing the respect that they may have had for each other. The parent is forced to choose between siding with the teacher or with her own child. While this may not be a significant problem with older students who have established a reputation with the parents, with younger children this can cause an uncomfortable dilemma for the parent. Ultimately, it is certainly not a situation conducive to a positive relationship between the parties.

The solution is to always have the student present at the conference. This will ensure that all of the information is out in the open, and that stories cannot be altered. It also gives you an opportunity to demonstrate to the parent that you *do* respect the child, but that you are holding the child accountable for behaviors and academic progress. Remember, one of the primary reasons that parents lose respect for the teacher is through the belief that the teacher is unfair to their child. Having the child present for the majority of the conference can alleviate that problem.

■ **Actively limit any prejudice, ethnocentrism, or stereotyping.** Be very careful not to fall into the trap that many teachers experience—prejudicing the parents of the school. Prejudice does not mean the same as racism. It means judging parents based on their general ethnocentric or socioeconomic qualities before you get to know them. For example, being at a high socioeconomic "white" school does not mean the parents are automatically involved and supportive. Conversely, it does not mean that they will be "problems" and should be treated with caution.

Being at a lower socioeconomic "immigrant" school does not mean that the parents are automatically noncaring. They may not be financially able to take off from work and come in to conferences and other programs. It does not mean that they do not care. Nor does a parent's limited English ability have any correlation with her concern for her child's education.

As a matter of respect, watch for these types of prejudice, ethnocentrism, or stereotyping. To do otherwise, you immediately become disrespectful. Ultimately, if you foster respect for the parent, you will be respected in return and a true partnership will develop—one that will lead to greater achievement for the child.

For the Parent

- **Use proper channels for problems.** How would you feel if your employees or customers at work went over your head to your boss to complain about you every time a problem developed? You would probably feel that it was extremely disrespectful, and it would surely feed negative feelings toward that party. When parents complain to a teacher's superior, the teacher feels the same way and will react the same way.

  If you have a problem with a teacher—something that was said or done—the worst thing you can do is go directly to the principal about it. Yes, you may get satisfaction and have the problem immediately resolved. However, even if you win, you lose. There are few things that upset teachers more than a parent going over their head without first talking to them to find a resolution. By disregarding this first step, you have immediately destroyed your relationship with that teacher. There is no way that teacher will respect you, much less trust you, after this type of action. As a result, no partnership will ever exist between the two of you.

  If you have a problem with something the teacher did or said, as a first step, contact the teacher and ask about it. (Obviously, I am not talking about extremely serious offences such as child abuse.) This is not to say that the parent's concern is not legitimate! Quite the contrary—in virtually every scenario, the parent's perceptions at the time are a cause for concern.

However, it has been my experience that most of the time, one of the following will occur when the parent goes to the teacher first:

- The parent realizes that there was a miscommunication or misperception, which is quickly resolved.
- The parent realizes that the child actively lied or misrepresented the teacher.
- The teacher realizes that a mistake was made, or that something was not explained or said the way it was intended. Apologies are made, and the situation is corrected.

In all of these scenarios, a legitimate concern is rectified by simply talking to the teacher. No disrespect is made by immediately going over the teacher's head. No negative feelings develop toward the parent. And more important, the problem is resolved.

However, if after discussing your concerns with the teacher you feel the problem has not been adequately resolved, at that point it is time to take the matter further. You need to ascertain who is that teacher's supervising administrator. In a small elementary school, it may be the school principal. In large schools and those on the secondary level, it will most likely be an assistant principal, a magnet coordinator, or a department head. In any event, you need to move to the next immediate level for the same reasons that you do not want to go over the teacher's head initially.

If you have legitimate concerns, you will eventually get satisfaction. It may take a little longer to go through appropriate channels to resolve your concerns. However, by doing so you will maintain a respectful relationship with the involved parties—even if they may disagree with you. They will observe that you were not trying to cause them trouble, and that you respected them enough to attempt a resolution first.

■ **Be realistic about your child.** All parents want their child to be the best; all parents want their child to succeed. It is natural for parents to primarily see the good in their child and to attribute any bad qualities to outside forces or individuals. Unfortunately, this directly leads to the issue of respect. Remember the discussion earlier in this chapter that respect disappears when a parent feels that the child was treated unfairly. If your expectations of your child are not realistic, or at least skewed, then you will eventually be faced with a situation where you will feel that your child was treated unfairly.

As far as the level of academic achievement for your child, do some investigation on your own. Study the different levels of papers posted in the classroom. Ask the teacher to show you some examples of exemplary work (names can be covered or removed easily). Then compare this work with your child's. Now you can make a comparison. Where does your child fit in? Top, bottom, average? This activity will immediately provide you with a more realistic view of your child's achievement.

The same is true with your child's behavior. If you have behavioral concerns, you should occasionally visit the school during the morning or lunch breaks and observe the students. Learn about the types of behaviors demonstrated by students your child's age. Behaviors demonstrated with peers at school is often quite different than that demonstrated at home. Once again, through this type of observation, you can get a better perspective of your child's behaviors.

Finally, listen to your child's teacher. Ask for specifics. Ask where the deficiencies arise and how they can be rectified. Having a child who is experiencing difficulties is not the problem—not realizing the causes and possible solutions becomes the problem. Being realistic about your child's abilities and deficiencies is directly related to a respectful partnership between you and the teacher.

■ **You teach your child respect by example.** Ultimately, the respect or disrespect you demonstrate toward the teacher or school is learned by your child. This can be as blatant as referring to the teacher with derogatory or nasty language in your child's presence, even if you are talking to another adult. This particular type of behavior is dangerous because it negatively empowers the child. The next time there is any type of confrontation between the two, your child will most likely feel that you will automatically take his side against the teacher.

Disrespect can also be taught in subtle ways. Anytime that you lie for your child to help her get out of trouble, such as writing a false excuse for a missing assignment, you teach a message about a lack of respect for the teacher. Lying to the teacher to save yourself embarrassment, such as when you let your child miss school for a social reason or as a convenience for you, also sends the identical message. That does not mean that you should never take your child out of school for those reasons. Just be honest with the teacher as to your reason, and let your child observe this honesty. Be careful—children will listen to what you say and do, and they will learn.

Ultimately, if you foster respect for the teacher, you will get the respect back, and a true partnership will develop, one that will lead to greater achievement for the child.

Bibliography

Armstrong, T. *Multiple Intelligences in the Classroom.* 2nd ed. Alexandria, VA: Association for Supervision and Curriculum Development, 2000.

ASCD SmartBrief. ascd@smartbrief.com. E-mail newsletter. September 12, 2006. Alexandria, VA: Association for Supervision and Curriculum Development, 2006.

Baker, A. J. and L. M. Soden. *The Challenges of Parent Involvement Research.* New York: ERIC Clearinghouse on Urban Education (ERIC Document reproduction Service No. ED 419 030), 1998.

Bloom, B. S., ed. *Taxonomy of Educational Objectives: Handbook I: Cognitive Domain.* New York: David McKay, 1953.

Carlson, C. G. *The Parent Principle: Prerequisite for Educational Success.* (Rep. No. PS 019854) Princeton, NJ: Educational Testing Service (ERIC Document Reproduction Service No. ED 337 278), 1991.

Chapin, H. *Cat's in the Cradle.* Verities & Balderdash: Elektra Records, 1974.

Epstein, J. L. *School/Family/Community Partnerships: Caring for the Children We Share.* Phi Delta Kappan, 76(9), 701–712, 1995.

Epstein, J. L. *School, Family and Community Partnerships: Preparing Educators and Improving Schools.* Boulder, CO: Westview Press, 2001.

Ferguson, C. *Developing a Collaborative Team Approach to Support Family and Community Connections with Schools: What Can School Leaders Do?* Austin, TX: Southwest Educational Development Laboratory, 2005.

Floyd, L. *Joining Hands: A Parental Involvement Program.* Urban Education, 33(1), 123–135, 1998.

Garfield, J. B. *Follow My Leader.* New York: Viking Press, 1957.

Gibbs, N. "Parents behaving badly." *Time,* February 21, 2005, 41–49.

Gomez, R. and R. Greenough. *Parent Involvement Under the New Title I and Title III: From Compliance to Effective Practice.* Unpublished manuscript, Northwest Regional Educational Laboratory, Portland, OR, 2002.

Josephson, M. *Character Counts.* Los Angeles: Josephson Institute of Ethics, 1993.

Mandel, S. *Cybertrips in Social Studies: Online Field Trips for All Ages.* Chicago: Zephyr Press, 2002.

Mandel, S. *Cooperative Work Groups: Preparing Students for the Real World.* Tuscon: Corwin Press, 2003.

Mandel, S. *Improving Test Scores: A Practical Approach for Teachers and Administrators.* Chicago: Zephyr Press, 2006a.

Mandel, S. "Teachers and parents: A partnership for student achievement questionnaire." Unpublished questionnaire, available from author, 2006b.

Macfarlane, E. C. *Children's Literacy Development: Suggestions for Parent Involvement.* ERIC Digest #ED 365979, 1994.

MetLife Survey of the American Teacher. *Transitions and the Role of Supportive Relationships: A Survey of Teachers, Principals and Students.* Harris Interactive Inc., 2005.

National Education Longitudinal Study. Washington, D.C.: National Center for Educational Statistics, 1988.

National PTA. *National Standards for Parent/Family Involvement Programs.* Chicago, IL: 1998.

National PTA. *Building Successful Partnerships: A Guide for Developing Parent and Family Involvement Programs.* Bloomington, IN: National Educational Service, 2000.

Spurlock, M. (2004). *Super Size Me: Educationally Enhanced Movie Edition.* Roadside Attractions Productions.

Tellin' Stories Project Action Research Group. *Between Families and Schools: Creating Meaningful Relationships.* Washington, D.C.: Network for Educators on the Americas, Tellin' Stories Project, 2000.

Index